THE NORTHWESTERN UNITED STATES

THE NORTHWESTERN UNITED STATES

CHARLES W. BOOTH

Eastern Washington State College

A SEARCHLIGHT ORIGINAL

under the general editorship of

G. ETZEL PEARCY

Chairman, Department
of Geography, California State
College at Los Angeles

GEORGE W. HOFFMAN

Professor of Geography
University of Texas

VAN NOSTRAND REINHOLD COMPANY

New York   Cincinnati   Toronto   London   Melbourne

Preface

THIS book is a description and analysis of the features of the Pacific Northwest that contribute most forcefully to the character of the region. An area easily defined by directions, the region is the northwestern corner of the contiguous United States, comprising the states of Washington, Oregon, Idaho and western Montana.

After a general overview of the region, the physical and economic aspects of regional significance are reviewed. A plan to present the principal elements involved in the interaction of the physical and cultural environments begins here and continues throughout the remaining chapters, giving the book a human geography bias.

The writer Wallace Stegner has said that "comparatively, the Pacific Northwest is still in the state of innocence." This state of innocence manifests itself in several ways, ranging from economic development to social and political phenomena. Comparatively, the region is untouched. A strong territorial affection exists between the people and their landscape, and the urge to live in, but at the same time preserve the natural beauty of the region, has produced an extremely conservation-minded populace. Apparently, the understanding that the "great outdoors" is truly just out the door has produced an unsigned covenant for its continuance.

There is a certain innocence, too, in the sense that the region has little in the way of tradition. There is no counterpart in the Northwest to the long-standing family yacht club memberships of New England or the numerous characteristically "southern" traditions. There are not even the strong ties with the tradition of religion, as Washington and Oregon ranked the lowest amongst all the states in church affiliation as late as the mid 1960s.

Politically, the state of innocence should be viewed benevolently for youthful, blissful ignorance has probably been responsible for such past behavior as the 1886 raid on Chinatown in Seattle, when most of its residents were sent back to the Orient on the good ship *Queen of the Pacific*. Further indulgence of its adolescent innocence may be required to understand the relatively late enactment of laws relating to public accommodations and child labor. However, while time, in the most simple chronological sense, may be an important factor in explaining the relatively late arrival of a political and social consciousness that goes beyond rugged individualism, it should not be inferred that the region is entirely within a state of social infancy.

While the frontier threshold has moved on to Alaska, experiences fresh in the minds of comparatively young men reveal its passing has been a matter of only a few years. New towns have sprung up where the moving frontier had left civilizational voids—places like the Mission Valley, south of Flathead Lake in Montana, have been opened for settlement as recently as 1910. The imprint of man on this northwestern land is as fresh as the landscape itself, and the projects devised to cause it to issue forth its promise are a tribute to the imagination and tenacity of their planners.

So, comparatively, the region is youthful and innocent, but the pressures of its developmental schemes are becoming stronger forces in sculpting the region's character. The telescoping effects of industrial innovation and general economic growth will no doubt propel some parts of the region faster than they wish to go, indeed, such is already the case with the Puget Sound area. Owing to the nature of the Pacific Northwest, parts of it will remain innocent for some time to come, but the region appears to have at least achieved the threshold for a general state of regional maturity.

Most men's perspective probably begins with someone else's and this writer is no exception. The faults that exist in these pages are surely my responsibility, but I wish to acknowledge the fact that my father, friends and teachers have all been important influences in my perception of land and life in the Northwest.

CHARLES W. BOOTH

Contents

Tables

Maps (following p. 56)

1   *A Geographic Overview*

The Northwestern States, or the Pacific Northwest, as the area is more commonly called, is a region of tremendous physical diversity. The cool, moist, marine environment of its Pacific face gives way to desert climates in the interior. The rugged alpine wilderness of its mountain environments contrasts sharply with the extensive prairies of the intermontane region. An extratropical rainforest, unique to the continent, stands isolated on the western Olympic Peninsula, while drab sagebrush lands spread themselves over the vast interiors of three states. A tabular basalt platform comprising an intermontane region, scarred by channels eroded by Pleistocene glacial floodwaters, is flanked by mountains whose structure reveals complex folding and faulting. Volcanic peaks dot the crest of the Cascade Mountains, while ancient fossils repose atop the Rockies.

The states of Washington, Oregon, and Idaho comprise the main body of this region, with the western flank of the Rocky Mountains of Montana providing the remainder. To geographers, the great drainage basin of the Columbia River is the factor which denotes its regional character. While such a criteria for regionalization does not correspond to the political boundaries of the states, it nevertheless provides a focal point which emphasizes the region's greatest natural asset.

The entire Pacific Northwest is encompassed by the great western cordilleran region of North America. The north-south trending Cascade and Rocky Mountain systems are the most spectacular and thus dominant physiographic features, although the Columbia Plateau vies for those honors by virtue of its size.

1

In general, the age of the major events in the region's tectonic past proceed from youngest to oldest in an easterly direction from the Pacific Coast to the Rocky Mountains. The Cascade Mountains are a part of the mountain system which extends the entire length of western North and South America. Igneous activity has been an important phase in the morphology of the Cascade landscape with perhaps the most impressive occurrence being the cataclysmic production of the caldera of Mount Mazama or Crater Lake as it is more commonly known. The ash debris from this explosive event in Oregon can be traced in a northwesterly direction from its source all the way to northern Idaho. By means of radio-carbon dating, these deposits have been ascertained as being between 6,000 and 7,000 years old. A similar but lesser explosive event occurred in conjunction with Glacier Peak, a volcano of the North Cascade region in Washington. The ash deposit from this disturbance has been found to pre-date the Mazama ash by approximately 6,000 years, but it is not as widespread in its distribution. These two deposits provide an extremely useful time benchmark, as it were, for the determination of the age of many other geological and anthropological occurrences in the region.

The tri-state intermontane region comprises one of the most massive basalt extrusion formations in the world. Extruded from vents and fissures within the area itself, this Columbia Plateau lava material covers an expanse of over 200,000 square miles within the states of Washington, Oregon and Idaho. This phenomenon consists of numerous, essentially flat-lying flows of basalt which vary considerably in their vertical dimension. These flows buried an older surface of considerable local relief which is thought to have resembled the Basin and Range topography of northern California and Nevada.

Like the Cascades, the Rocky Mountains of this region are only a part of a larger uplifted mass having continental proportions. From Alaska to Mexico, the Rockies are testimony to large scale orogeny over a long period of time. This building process has produced one of the few outstanding scenic recreational areas of the

North American continent. Wallace Atwood, an American physiographer, spoke of them as having colors "comparable in brilliancy to the autumn tints of the Eastern decidous forests."

Since the time of the Lewis and Clark expedition to the Far West, this northwestern region has reveled in its characterization as a land of great beauty—a region abounding in the environmental gifts of God. People who live east of the Mississippi still recall it as "God's Country." Such a characterization is exaggerated, of course. There are great stretches of the intermontane region that hardly resemble one's notion of a gift of God. While Washington chooses as its motto "The Evergreen State," that euphemism can actually be applied to only slightly better than one-third of its territory. Be that as it may, the landscape of this country does merit at least a modicum of the praise that was expressed by its early explorers.

Along with its characteristics of beauty and physical diversity, the region also exhibits the traits of youth. Historically speaking, the region's youthful state is revealed by the following comparisons: In 1775, Heceta, from the Spanish ship "Santiago," landed at Point Grenville near Grays Harbor, Washington—the same year as the battles of Lexington and Bunker Hill. Alexander MacKenzie, the first explorer to traverse the continent along its greatest dimension, reached the shores of the Pacific in 1793, 186 years after the settlement of Jamestown.

Population statistics reveal that the census of 1850 found only 13,294 white people in the whole of the Oregon country, while the population of Missouri, the eastern terminus of the 2,000-mile Oregon Trail was 682,044. Ohio, Pennsylvania, Virginia, and Tennessee all had populations of over one million at that time. It is also true that here in the West during this period (1855) Indian reservations were being established to incarcerate the "savage" while the debates leading to a war to free the slaves were taking place in the Senate chambers in Washington, D. C.

The transition from the explorer-pioneer economic stage was largely brought about by the prospectors, lumbermen and farmers who founded the pattern of resource exploitation that dominated developmental history until 1941. Large public works projects administered by the Bureau of Reclamation and the Corps of Engineers were commenced during the Great Depression years. These projects further enhanced the possibilities for growth and when the Second World War years arrived, the region was ready for its next economic infusion. This latter period ushered in the present stage of industrial budding typified by a successful aircraft and aerospace manufacturer, a diversified forest products industry, a highly technical agricultural industry and attendant food processing, a growing chemicals industry, and significant recreational equipment manufacturing.

Regional Hindrances. Several facets of the region's character have been responsible for retarded regional development. In the realm of the physical environment, large segments of the area are dominated by either arid climates or mountainous terrain. Not only are these the least hospitable as settlement areas, but they have also acted as inhibiting factors to migration.

While the region's mountain systems provide the parent environment for the scenic wonderment of glaciers, evergreen vegetation and alpine lakes and streams, they also constitute approximately 75 percent of the total area of the region. In regard to the availability of land for conventional economic use then, the Pacific Northwest is comparable to the island domain of Japan, where approximately 25 percent of the land area is in plain. Approximately one-half of the land that might be suited for agricultural use by virtue of its soil and topographic conditions receives ten inches or less precipitation each year. The increased costs associated with the necessary irrigation land developments of this nature and the foreboding environment itself were inhibiting factors toward its development.

Lumbering and mining, the two industries that attracted the initial attention to the region, did not furnish a broad enough basis for either rapid or widespread settlement. Lumber processing was confined to the coastal regions where both the trees and transportation were accessible. Access to the interior of the region from any direction involved the rigors of breaching the mountains, despite the existence of the Columbia River. Prior to any improvements of this potential inland waterway its use was only seasonal and involved difficult portages.

Resource exploitation associated with mining and forestry, despite the prominence achieved by a few individuals, failed to produce the political power structure of some of the other regions of the United States. In contrast to the Eastern States, political figures from the Northwest have only recently become important characters of persuasion in the Congress of the United States (with the exceptions of Senator Borah of Idaho, and Dill of Washington.)

The combination of its embryonic political status, the frontier-like nature of its settlement and amenities, the extent of the geographic extremes in its environmental setting and the fact that the Pacific Northwest is not on the way to anywhere else have all been constraints on its growth and development.

2 *The Northwestern Situation: Locational and Physical Circumstances*

THERE IS a road sign on U.S. Highway 2 a few miles west of Kalispell, Montana, which reads, "Game Crossing, Next 78 miles." It is 1600 miles from Seattle to Chicago, and 750 miles to San Francisco. Over one-third of the region's outbound commodities travel distances of 1500 miles or more to their destinations. These are internal and external spatial facts of life for the Pacific Northwest.

While air travel literally has the effect of folding up the vast distances which separate this region from the rest of the United States, it has contributed only slightly to the breaking down of the spatial barrier between the area and the political and economic centers with which it must deal. The economic significance of distance must be considered a major factor in the developmental history of the region.

Hemmed in by mountains to the north and east, and desert and mountains to the south, the region has been effectively isolated from the main stream of western settlement. Add to this the physical nature of the region itself—85 percent of it suitable for forestry and grazing, 15 percent suitable for cultivation—and inducements for early settlement must have seemed slim indeed. Aside from those extractive industries which could exploit the natural resources of the region, very little was possible in the way of enhancing internal growth. In a manner of speaking, economic expansion has been

6

principally horizontal in its spatial dimension, having a vertical component in those places that were connected in some manner with the centers of resource exploitation of an extractive nature. As transportation systems evolved, a gradual filling in of the voids began to occur, but lands and resources having high social costs of development that were beyond the financial capacity of industry and the state governments went undeveloped until the capital resources of the federal government could be applied. This particular aspect of regional economic development will be explored in greater detail in the second part of this chapter and in Chapter 4. Suffice it to say here, the region's relative location with respect to its trade partners, its "out of sight, out of mind" communication problem with the seat of government, and the large intervening spaces between local commercial centers have been major elements in the logistical problem of regional development.

ASPECTS OF THE PHYSICAL ENVIRONMENT

Two of the most important situational aspects of the Northwestern States are its location within the zone of the onshore westerly winds and the adjacent (relatively warm) water mass, the Pacific Ocean. In combination, these two factors exert a profound climatic influence on the region. The phenomena that result from these two climatic controls provides one of the best case studies of the interrelationships that exist between the various elements of our natural environment.

As a case in point, the lifting effect of the Coast Range, the Olympics, and the Cascade Mountains in causing windward side orographic precipitation is virtually a textbook example of that process. The moisture laden onshore surface winds and cyclonic storms are forced to rise by these obstacles and the resulting cooling causes the condensation necessary for precipitation. The operation of this combination of factors is so widespread and recurrent in nature that it goes far beyond just providing the western portions of Washington and Oregon with an affluence of moisture. The subsequent depletion of water vapor plus the tendency for the moving air to descend and warm on the leeward mountain sides is antithetical to the processes which cause precipitation. A drastic reduction in moisture availability is caused and the phenomenon of a "rain shadow" results. This is particularly true in the case of the Olympics, causing the apparent anachronism of a place receiving an annual amount of 16 inches of precipitation being only 40 miles from one which receives over 140 inches per year. (See Figure 2.) The Coast Range is not sufficiently high to cause such an exaggerated climatic influence to the leeward.

Needless to say, the precipitation, natural vegetation, and zonal soils exist in their expected patterns of interdependence in the Northwestern States and if one learns the principal causative factors which include the amount and distribution pattern of the precipitation, the rest becomes an exercise in association, though perhaps not as simple a procedure as it may sound.

In addition to its importance as a source region for water vapor, winds and storms, the Eastern Pacific also plays a vital role in the temperature characteristics of the region. Warmer in winter, cooler in summer, western Washington and Oregon have milder climates than their continental counterparts of the same latitude. This moderating marine influence declines eastward, yet persists to the extent that the climate of the area east of the Cascades is not as extreme as that of the Great Plains. The effects of continentality do not predominate in the climatic patterns of the Pacific Northwest until one passes the front wall and encounters the middle portions of the Rocky Mountains. It is at this juncture that the precipitation regime of a winter maximum nurtured by the marine influence and cyclonic storms is reversed and the continental influence is more prevalent.

It can be seen that the marine influence, prevailing winds, and cyclonic storms in concert with the orography of the region are elements of a fundamental nature in the geographic circumstances of the Northwestern States.

PHYSIOGRAPHIC REGIONS

As noted earlier, the most prominent physiographic features of the region are parts of the larger geomorphic pattern of the North American continent. The two essentially parallel mountain ranges of the Cascades and Rockies divide the region into four main units: the two mountain systems themselves, the large area between them, and the Pacific coastal region.

Figure 3, which depicts the physiographic regions of the Pacific Northwest, is a simplified version of a more detailed study done earlier by Professor Otis Freeman and associates.[1]

PACIFIC BORDER

From the Cascade Mountains to the west there are five major regions sharing in common the climatic phenomena of the marine influence of the Pacific Ocean.

Olympic Highlands. The Olympic Highlands constitutes a glaciated mountainous massif, heavily forested at the lower elevations but reaching far beyond the tree line with peaks barren except for year round snow cover. Mount Olympus is the highest peak, having an elevation of 7,915 feet above sea level. Some slopes on the western side receive as much as 150 inches of precipitation a year, which has been an important environmental factor in producing a temperate climate rainforest there. This region rivals the Northern Rockies in its alpine beauty and would make a fine setting for the second awakening of Rip Van Winkle. This environment is primeval in the truest sense of the word and the establishment of Olympic National Park in 1938 is an assurance of its perpetuation.

Willamette-Puget Lowlands. This lowland region is essentially a trough extending approximately 350 miles from Puget Sound on

[1] Otis Freeman and Howard Martin, *The Pacific Northwest* (New York: Wiley & Company, 1954).

the north to Eugene, Oregon, to the south. It contains all but one of the entire Northwestern States' metropolitan areas with populations over 50,000 and is destined to remain the principal area of population settlement and growth. Glaciation has been a prominent force in the configuration of the Puget Sound, whereas the physical character of the Willamette Valley has been strongly influenced by both past and present fluvial action.

While the Puget Sound area is oriented toward commerce, manufacturing and transportation, the Willamette Valley is noted for its agricultural and lumber industries. Portland at the northern end of the Willamette Valley on the Columbia River is rapidly establishing itself as the second most important port of the Pacific coast (after Los Angeles). The Puget Sound region is one of the nation's most scenic metropolitan settings and Seattlites are justified in the pride they have of their view of Mount Rainier across Lake Washington and the jagged peaks of the Olympics beyond the Sound. They have also developed some compensatory attitudes, however. "Measurable precipitation" and "marine air" are two overworked terms invoked to reduce the significance of the rather constant wetness encountered during the cool season.

The Coast Range. The Coast Range extends from the Klamath Highlands on the south to Grays Harbor on the north—a distance of approximately 250 miles. This range has an average crest line elevation of approximately 1,500 feet. While the elevations are not comparable to the Cascades or Olympics (highest is Marys Peak at 4,097 feet), they are sufficient to trigger the mechanism of orographic precipitation. The copious precipitation is a major factor in the growth of a large Douglas Fir forest resulting quite naturally in the region becoming an important center for the lumber industry of Oregon. Accessibility to the forest by way of lowland and coastal water transportation routes and rapid tree growth are significant factors in this location. Seaward, a narrow coastal fringe containing numerous bays and inlets represents an important recreational area as well as providing the base for a small fishing industry of which Coos Bay is the center. In many of these coastal areas in Oregon, dairying is an important enterprise: the Tillamook region is an example of an area which has achieved national fame. On the eastern side, the Range gradually decreases in dimension to foothills that grade into the Willamette Valley.

Klamath Highlands. The Klamath Highlands lie in the southwestern corner of Oregon between the Cascades and the sea, and to the south of the Coast Range. It is a rugged area topographically with local relief varying from 2,000 to 5,000 feet. Its structure and erosional history are quite complex. One of its most interesting geomorphic aspects is the manner in which its mountain tops are generally rounded, while the nature of the lower elevational areas is one of steep-walled canyons and valleys—an indication of the production of an older erosional surface, then further uplift and a resumption of downcutting by the local streams.

The region is sparsely settled, the towns being located on the inland transportation lines leading south to California. The coastal lowland is very narrow with cliffs and rock abutments adjacent to the sea for the most part. The Rogue River valley is the most prominent area of settlement, supporting irrigation agriculture and producing the famed "Royal Riviera" pear. Southern Oregon College at Ashland produces an annual Shakespearean Festival, so despite the appearance to the outsider of an isolated mountain country environment, the region is not entirely culturally deprived.

Cascade Mountains. The Cascade Mountains extend 500 miles—the full length of both Washington and Oregon and, as previously mentioned, into Canada, California and beyond. Their width varies, but as a generalization they are wider in the north (100 miles), narrowing as they progress southward. (Their width is approximately 50 miles at the southern margin of the region.) Most of the prominent peaks are near the 10,000-foot mark. Famous Mount

Rainier at 14,407 feet is the highest. Alpine glaciation is a major feature of both the scenery and the processes associated with the configuration of the landscape.

This relatively small portion of the great Eastern Pacific cordillera is of great significance to the region. In short, it comprises far more than the sum of its most obvious parts—mountain peaks, snow, trees, lakes and streams. As a forested area it serves as an important source of lumber and wildlife. As a watershed it supplies water for domestic purposes, hydroelectric power and irrigation. As a beautiful wilderness it serves the recreational aspirations of the hunter, skier, camper, fisherman and hiker. There are two National Parks in the Cascades: Crater Lake in Oregon and Mount Rainier in Washington (with the possibility of a third, North Cascades, in Washington in the near future). State Parks and Forest Service recreational areas are too numerous to mention. The close proximity of the Cascades to the Willamette-Puget population node is an important factor in the recreational schema of these people. The Cascades also represent a social dividing line almost equal to the differences in climate they produce—a subject to be pursued later in this chapter.

EASTERN PHYSIOGRAPHIC REGIONS

East of the Cascades there are nine major geomorphic units, at least one of which (Columbia Plateau) has numerous subdivisions which will not be discussed here.

Okanogan-Selkirk Highlands. This region lies to the north of the Columbia and Spokane Rivers, east of the Cascades, and west of the Purcell Trench in Idaho. For all practical purposes, Pend Oreille, Stevens, Ferry, and Okanogan counties in Washington embrace all of the region except the small portion which is in Idaho. Seven north-south trending valleys (the Methow, Okanogan, San Poil, Columbia-Kettle River, Colville, Pend Oreille and Priest), with similar trending mountainous ranges in between, constitute the basic pattern of the topography.

The area contains stump ranches (small grazing and farm lots produced by cutting timber, but leaving the stumps), small to medium sized sawmills, three Indian reservations, and a few mines of local significance producing gold, lead, silver, zinc, limestone, magnesite and uranium. Approximately one-half of the area is within the boundaries of three National Forests. There are a few towns in the valleys, none of which has a population over 3,000. The Okanogan Valley is one of the major apple growing sites in Washington. An important recreational area, this entire region contains numerous lakes whose fish populations are maintained by the Washington State Game Commission. Big game hunting is avidly pursued here and Stevens County is perennially at or near the top of the hunter success statistics for deer in the state.

The four counties previously mentioned are almost constantly plagued with unemployment problems and have qualified for project funds distributed by the Area Redevelopment Administration for some time. (See figure 4.) This was Goldwater Country during that brief era and represented a stronghold of conservative political opinion. "Impeach Earl Warren" signs can still be seen around the countryside.

Columbia Plateau. One of the most outstanding physical aspects of this region is an immense basalt platform consisting of numerous flows originating from sources other than volcanoes within the area covered by the flows themselves. The depth of this material is known to be over 10,000 feet in the Pasco Basin, and where the Columbia and Snake Rivers have been responsible for dissection, spectacular gorges and attendant landforms have evolved. The northern half of this area has been greatly modified by glacial floodwaters of immense proportions resulting in the "Channeled Scabland" topography described by J. Harlan Bretz.[2] Grand Coulee, one of the

[2] Bretz, J. Harlan, *Washington's Channeled Scablands,* Bulletin 45 (Olympia, Washington: 1959). Division of Mines and Geology, Department of Conservation, 1959). See also "The Channeled Scablands of the Columbia Plateau," *Journal of Geology,* vol. 31, 8, (Nov.–Dec., 1923).

largest channels created by this erosional process, is now utilized as a reservoir for irrigation water for the Columbia Basin Irrigation Project, which is located in the central portion of the region.

This plateau area is the most northerly portion of an intermontane region which extends to the southern Oregon boundary and to the eastern end of the Snake River valley. Even considering its size, the Columbia Plateau displays a great deal of diversity. It contains the erosional scars of the Channeled Scablands, three Bureau of Reclamation Irrigation Projects (Columbia Basin, Umatilla and Yakima Valley), one of the most productive dryland wheat areas of the world (the Palouse region), a series of folded formations called the Yakima Folds, and the gorge of the Columbia River.

This entire region has been considerably modified in the sense of physical change. For example, the numerous irrigation projects have transformed large areas of raw sagebrush land into gargantuan gardens. Grand Coulee Dam, the key to the largest part of this transformation, is located on the northern rim of this area. The dryland wheat farmers of the southern slopes of the region (Horse Heaven Hills) have even modified the natural climatic environment by employing cloud seeding to increase moisture availability for their crops.

The archaeological site of the Marmes Rockshelter is located within this region near the confluence of the Palouse and Snake Rivers. Identified initially as a likely location for Indian artifacts, the project was one of several investigations in that area. After excavations reached deeply into the underlying strata, however, human remains of an older cultural group were unearthed. The importance of this site stems from the fact that the older remains from this site of antiquity are among the oldest on the North American continent. It is also an unusual site in that the chronology of past events, both human and natural, can be reconstructed with a good deal of accuracy. The volcanic ash described in Chapter One played an important role in the dating of events and circumstances at this site. Unfortunately, the dig became inundated as a result of building the lower Monumental Dam on the Snake River.

The Tri-Cities of Pasco, Kennewick and Richland, located in the south-central portion of the region along the Columbia River, are undergoing very rapid growth associated with the burgeoning agricultural enterprises. Spokane is the largest metropolitan area in the region and the second largest city in the state of Washington. Located in the northeastern corner of this region it claims as its hinterland the "Inland Empire," which stretches west to Yakima, east to Missoula, Montana, south to the Tri-Cities and Lewiston, Idaho, and north through the whole of the Okanogan-Selkirk Highlands. Spokane's original importance as a mountain gateway transportation center has declined over the years as other elements of its economy expanded, but the transportation industry will probably become a dominant feature in its existence again as technological changes occur in that industry and larger trade markets appear in Japan and other Asian countries. (See Chapter 6.)

Central Highlands. This mountainous area of north-central Oregon, like others of its kind in the Northwest, owes its original settlement to gold fever and an overland trail. It contains two main mountain systems, the Wallowas and Blues, the latter containing no less than nine smaller ranges varying in elevation from 3,000 to 9,000 feet. The whole of the region is severely eroded, with alpine glaciation being responsible for the extent of local relief in the Wallowas. The eastern edge of this area is bounded by the great canyon of the Snake River, the most notable part of which is the 6,000-foot-deep Hells Canyon.

The watershed of these mountains provides irrigation water for agriculture in the interior basins and valleys and a kind of transhumance is still practiced as the upland pastures continue to be used for the summer grazing of cattle and sheep. The pine forest of the region also provides the basis for a lumber industry of local importance.

Like the Okanogan Highlands of Washington, this region is a population void for the most part with the exception of Baker, a town of 10,000 located on the old Oregon Trail.

Placer gold, silver, mercury, chromite and copper all exist within the region and were important motivations for early settlement. As in many other territories of the Northwest, most of the original mining settlements withered into ghost towns and are now old and weather-beaten relics—symbols of an era for which some Westerners still mourn.

Harney High Plains and Malheur Basin. The large area which comprises these regions is in sharp contrast to the other areas previously discussed. The climate is decidedly semi-arid. Water is scarce, vegetation sparse. Playa lakes and alkali flats are scattered throughout and, for most who view it, it simply is a God-forsaken place. However, in its own special way, it is as much a wild area as a forest wilderness is.

The large ranches of the Malheur country count their acres by the thousands as huge parcels of land are required to provide an economic grazing unit. In the late 1800s Pete French, one of this region's most famous men, operated a cattle spread that extended from near the edge of the Steens Mountains to Malheur Lake, a distance of 70 miles. When he met his death by gunshot in the true western fashion, his ranch contained 250,000 acres and perhaps as many as 20,000 head of cattle. The Harney Country (Malheur Basin) was a part of the authentic West, providing a backdrop for the two western plots of cowboys against Indians and the ranchers against the settling farmers. The cowboys were called "Buckaroos" here and they had trouble with the Piaute and Bannock Indians as late as 1878.

The Harney High Plains has volcanic cinder cones scattered about in its western portion. Otherwise the region is without much topographical diversity. The lava flows are deemed to be very young in age, perhaps occurring after the last ice age. Thinking that there are similarities between this surface and that of the moon, the area has been used as an orientation model for prospective moon travellers by the National Aeronautical and Space Administration.

The Malheur Basin is a region of interior drainage with the

Harney and Malheur Lake depressions being the principal recipients of what little water reaches the area. The amount of water in these basins varies greatly, although Malheur Lake is partially regulated since it is now a national wildlife refuge. The town of Burns, named after the poet Robert Burns by one of its early founders, is the supply center for a large part of this southeastern Oregon area.

Basin and Range and Owyhee Tableland. The Basin and Range regions in Oregon and Idaho constitute the northern segments of the larger physiographic region of Nevada and Utah. The alignment of the topography is in a generally north-south direction. This is a rugged country, sharing the climatic and vegetation pattern of its northern neighbor but having far greater relief. The Steens Mountains, for example, a fault block structure, rise abruptly over 5,000 feet from the floor of the Alvord Desert to an elevation of 9,600 feet. Some of the basins which alternate with these short mountainous ranges contain large shallow lakes. The landform features of this region are extremely sharp owing to the dry climate and resulting slow erosion. Spring comes late to this area, with frost sometimes occurring in every month of the year. Grazing is the predominant economic activity.

The Owyhee Tableland is a maturally dissected region. Its well-established drainage pattern is in sharp contrast to that of the Basin and Range or Malheur Basin regions, with several smaller streams being directly tributary to the Snake River. The Owyhee River and its tributaries join the Snake after they have sculptured the southwestern portion of the region. This is the last of the four southern regions of the Northwest which share the common characteristics of aridity, a grazing economy, and population vacuums. The population densities of these regions is less than two people per square mile and nearly a hundred acres per year per animal are required for cattle grazing. Except for the eastern and western edges of this large four-region area, it is without the services of rail transportation, since no line traverses it. As might be expected, the highway network (using the term loosely) serves the purpose of connecting intra-regional service centers and transporting people through the region—most of them as rapidly as possible.

Snake River Plain. Irrigation agriculture, based on development by the Bureau of Reclamation, is the most outstanding feature of this region. The large arc described by the Snake River and its flood-plain has been a favored settlement region because of the long growing season, adaptable soils, and accessibility to large quantities of good water. Some of the early gold discoveries were located along the northern edge of the middle and western portions of the Snake River, bringing attention to the area as something more than a "passing through country," and contributing to its early settlement.

The seemingly endless basalt platform of the Pacific Northwest occupies this region too, but it finally ends along the southern and western margins of the Rocky Mountains which border the plain. Away from the rivers and irrigation projects the area is every bit as dry and desolate as the Harney High Plains or Malheur Basin. Practically all of the towns are agriculturally oriented as even Boise, the state capital and largest city of the state of Idaho, is also the local headquarters of the Bureau of Reclamation. Pocatello on the southeastern margin is an exception to this generalization for it is an important mountain gateway transportation center.

Rocky Mountains. The Rocky Mountains constitute almost one-third of the total area of the Pacific Northwest. The whole state of Idaho is identified with them and the western portion of Montana included in the Northwestern States is entirely dominated by them.

The Rockies are one of the oldest landform features of the Northwestern States and certainly one of the most scenic. Glacier National Park is an area of particular beauty about which even geologists speak of the almost architectural quality of the sculpting of the massive uplifted crustal blocks. Unlike the Cascades, volcanoes are not a prominent part of the highland physiography of the northern Rockies.

The Rocky Mountain region is by no means an homogeneous mass of uplifted and overturned earth crust. Numerous structural trenches (such as the Purcell, Clark Fork, and Flathead-Bitterroot) are distributed throughout the mountainous terrain of this region. It is within these trenches and companion valleys and basins that the economic life of the region is gradually being extended and diversified.

Mineral deposits are scattered throughout the Rockies and those places that are limited by the natural environment to the exploitation of the minerals and little else still personify the "boom or bust" mining character of the past. The smaller logging communities seem to reflect this character also. The further one is removed from "civilization," the more one confronts the past. Saturday night "stomps" are just what one expects them to be (with the exception that now the guitar is electrified).

The famous Coeur d'Alene mining district in the northern panhandle of Idaho has persevered as an area of significant mineral production since the early 1900s. Silver is of paramount interest here. Thus the recent manipulation of coinage requiring less silver content naturally raised some anguished voices. The general decline in the supply of silver and resulting price increase have considerably stimulated speculative interests, however, and the number of new claim applications in northern Idaho has all the characteristics of a land rush.

In the Montana Rockies, the cities of Butte and Anaconda are still significant in the production and processing of copper. However, a copper industry strike in 1967 was of such uncommon length that it plunged these cities into the "bust" portion of the mining cycle.

The northern Rockies are a principal watershed area of the Columbia Basin in the Northwestern States, producing streams such as the Snake, Salmon, Clearwater, Flathead, and Kootenai, all of which are important contributors to the hydroelectric power potential of the region. The attractiveness of the region has fostered a growing tourist and recreational enterprise.

Summary. By necessity, this has been an abbreviated description of the physiographic regions of the Pacific Northwest, but it should suffice to illustrate the extent of the environmental diversity that exists here. While a visitor to the region may be enthralled by the recreational power of the alpine wilderness, he must also be prepared to endure the heat and aridity of the intermontane region.

The human response to this environmental setting as evidenced by the major occupance patterns and economic endeavors will be a subject of later chapters.

GENERAL ECONOMIC CIRCUMSTANCES

Three ideas and three realities predominate in the general economic circumstances of the Pacific Northwest. The ideas are public works in the public domain for public welfare; regional planning; and conservation. The realities are an economy dominated by the extractive industries; economic immaturity; and divided state economies.

Public Works. Unquestionably, the most outstanding economic circumstance is the extent to which the federal government is involved in aiding the growth and development of this region. Direct and substantial federal economic support came early to this region in the form of Bonneville Dam, a public works project, during the depression years of the 1930s. This was the first in what has come to be a long line of government-sponsored water resource projects, stimulating the economy of the recipient region and those areas supplying ingredient elements as well. Even though the Pacific Northwest is still strongly oriented toward primary economic activities associated with the extractive industries, without the notion of public works the economic base and productivity would be far slimmer than it is.

The most important contribution of public works in the North-western States is within the sphere of hydroelectric power development. The region is practically devoid of mineral fuels and it has been evident from the outset that energy requirements would have to be met with hydroelectricity. While this observation was plain enough, it was not a simple matter to convince everyone of its authenticity as a solution to the problem of energy production. For example, when Grand Coulee Dam was being proposed as the second large federal project in the region and it was noted that besides supplying irrigation water it was going to create two million kilowatts of electrical power, a common retort was, "What are you going to do with all that electricity, put a light bulb in every rattlesnake hole?" (An apt description of the eastern Washington countryside at the time.)

The fact that this area probably contained the greatest hydroelectric potential in the United States and that a comprehensive plan would be required to insure complete integration of all facilities for optimum resource development no doubt had an influence on the decision to commence the undertaking by federal means. The possibilities inherent in this development did represent an attractive challenge to the politics of the New Deal and its economics. The Corps of Engineers and the Bureau of Reclamation, as construction agents of the federal government then, stand out as principal *dramatis personae* in the stimulation of economic development in the Northwestern States.

To use the public domain and its resources to advance the cause of public welfare was the seed from which the economy of the Northwestern States sprouted, and it has continued to be nurtured by that thought right up to the present time. One of the benefits of the democracy, the pooling of the nation's wealth, coupled with the idea of direct government participation in economic development, led to an accelerated and wider distribution of goods and services. In the Northwest this meant inexpensive electricity. It relieved rural hardships, increased productivity, which in turn increased disposable income, and, in general, tended to confer on the region's inhabitants a better means to participate in attaining the fruits of the nation's productive skills. It might be said that the manifestations of the public domain, public works, and public welfare in the Northwestern States have given substance to the words of Edmund Burke: "Government is a contrivance of human wisdom to provide for human wants. Men have a right that these wants should be provided by this wisdom."

Regional Planning. In 1931, while he was still Governor of New York, Franklin Roosevelt said, "In the long run, state and national planning is essential to the future prosperity, happiness and existence of the American people." The planning era resulting from his presidency commenced with the Public Works Administration's National Planning Board. In the Northwest, this Planning Board inaugurated an inventory of regional resources and laid the groundwork for river basin development. Since that time, four other planning agencies have been created, each with a greater degree of involvement. The Pacific Northwest Regional Planning Commission, the Columbia Interstate Compact Commission, Columbia Inter-Agency Commission and its successor the Pacific Northwest River Basins Commission represent an uninterrupted commitment to regional planning since 1934. It is redundant to point to the central role of water resource development in these planning agencies.

In addition to the planning functions carried out by these various commissions, the Corps of Engineers' "308 Report," [3] the Bureau of Reclamation's "Columbia River," [4] and the 1950 Report of the President's Water Resources Policy Commission all represent works of importance in planning for the utilization of the region's resources. The "308 Report" came to be the measure for nearly all proposals

---

[3] *Columbia River and Tributaries, Northwestern United States,* House Document #531, 81st Congress, 2nd Sesson (Washington, D.C.: U.S. Gov't. Printing Office, 1952).

[4] U.S. Department of the Interior. *The Columbia River* (Feb. 1947). Also Vol. 1, House Document #473, 1947.

for hydroelectric development throughout the entire Columbia River basin.

The Bonneville Power Administration, created in 1937 as the marketing agency for power produced from projects financed by public revenues, also has been involved in long-range planning in its projections for the consumption of hydroelectricity. This agency has most recently been engaged in the planning associated with the integration of nuclear energy generating sites into the electrical grid throughout the region. (See Figures 7 & 8.)

Conservation. Underlying the whole veneer of regional planning is the idea of conservation. While this word has been characterized as having "that excellent unifying quality of grand constitutional vagueness," [5] it can be defined in the Pacific Northwest by the practices that are associated with it. For example, in the forest, agricultural, and mineral industries it is characterized by the principle of planned depletion. In the forest preserves and recreational areas, compatible use and preservation are stressed. In the realm of water resources, conservation means comprehensive river basin development with a proclivity toward the integration of the multiple uses of power, irrigation, flood control, navigation, and recreation.

Tree farming, as an example of the sustained yield principle in the forest industry is termed "conservation" of which it is surely a type. While they are managed as game habitats, erosion control plots and watersheds in addition to their role as "tree gardens," there can be no denying the fact that tree farms are a reasonable means of perpetuating income from land that would otherwise become submarginal if it were not reforested. It is one of those cases where good management happily coincides with what the public conceives as conservation. Forest conservation practices, like all others, represent investments upon which there is a calculated return. No attempt is being made here to castigate the virtue of Smokey the Bear or de-

[5] Durning, Marvin B. "Challenge of Tomorrow," Keynote Address N.W.P.P.A. (Port Angeles, April 1966).

grade tree farms, but it is important to point out that forest conservation is good business as well as good business relations. After all, a tree farm is as a tree farm does.

In the field of recreation, preservation is playing a greater role in the northwestern conservation movement. The Sierra Club, a conservationist group that started in California, has been active and strident in the battles for the establishment and preservation of recreational space in the region. Convinced of the need for numerous and untouched wilderness preserves, its members have waged verbal war with foresters, mining companies and other potential competitors for wilderness areas.

There exists here a strong, almost unified commitment to the continuation of the environmental beauty of the region, and the husbanding aspect of the intelligent use of resources has been a dominant force in resource utilization. Perhaps it was inevitable that a region so dependent on an integrated plan for comprehensive and efficient water resource development would have strong motivations for a planning-conservation orientation.

The Realities. That the economy of the region is landscape oriented can be demonstrated in several ways. The regional income is dominated by agriculture, forestry, and recreation-tourism (usually in that order). The value of agricultural production for the state of Washington alone (approximately $809 million in 1969) is more than twice the value of mineral production in the whole of the Northwest.

Employment statistics reveal that trade, government, agriculture, services, lumber and transportation-communication utilities rank in that order in terms of labor force employment numbers. Of the rail carload tonnage originating in the Northwestern states (fifteen leading commodities) 70 percent is in the categories of forest, agricultural and mineral products.

With the exception of the Willamette-Puget Trough region the area is barely on its way toward economic sophistication and stability. Only approximately 20 percent of the labor force is utilized by *all* the forms of manufacturing, and the value added by manufacture, a useful index of secondary processing and integration, is only about $5 billion—less than a third of that of California.

In the Fall of 1962, one-third of the counties in the Northwestern States were eligible for accelerated public works programs under the auspices of the Area Redevelopment Administration. (See Figure 4.) Several areas that employ hand labor in various agricultural enterprises have cyclical unemployment problems that illustrate the lack of a diversified economic base and resultant depressed growth. For example, Okanogan County in Washington, an important apple growing area, often reaches a peak of 20 percent of its labor force in the unemployed ranks during the late summer months. This cyclical unemployment is also characteristic of the forest industries east of the Cascades during the winter months.

There are two areas of the Northwest that could be called anomalies insofar as this discussion of economic immaturity is concerned. The Seattle and Portland metropolitan areas are undergoing very rapid economic growth associated with the transportation industries. According to the Commission of Public Docks in Portland, its port is now second only to Los Angeles in total waterborne commerce handled, which makes it the number two Pacific Coast port. Ambitious plans for increased investment will provide even greater services and will no doubt be a stimulus for industrial growth in the Portland-Vancouver environs. Economic growth in the Seattle metropolitan area is primarily due to the Boeing Aircraft Corporation and other relations with the federal government. Approximately forty percent of the aircraft manufactured are sold to the government with the remaining going to commercial customers outside the region. Boeing is also involved in the aerospace industries and for two consecutive years (1966, 1967) has ranked third amongst the contractors to the National Aeronautics and Space Administration. The value of its contracts in 1967 ($273.5 million) was only slightly less than the value of mineral production in the Northwest.

Seattle is also the location of a specification center which aids in the distribution of information related to federal defense procurement activities. In 1967, Washington ranked 19th in amount of sales to the federal government for defense purposes. The three-state Pacific region (California, Oregon and Washington) ranks number one nationally in value of contracts with the Department of Defense. Curiously, this is a source of government largesse that is more or less unquestioned by those who decry the waste of other federal funds expended in programs whose design is to boost economic development and the level of support for social improvement.

This brings us to the third reality: the divided state economies. Many characteristics of the Northwestern States lend themselves to viewing the region as a more or less homogeneous unit, but nonetheless there is a discernible partitioning of each state. Washington is divided east and west along the Cascades, as is Oregon. Idaho is divided north and south by the Central Rockies.

In Washington, the eastern half is dominated by a rural agricultural economy while the west is characterized mainly by commerce and manufacturing. The western side also leans toward a liberal political view while the east reflects a more conservative attitude. Oregon is divided similarly (except for the political views). The Oregonians, odd as it may seem, tend in their Republicanism to be moderately conservative but elect maverick liberals such as Wayne Morse and Mark Hatfield. While Idaho is a "minerals north and an agricultural south," it is similar to Oregon in that its political ideals are fairly homogeneous on a statewide basis. The conservatism of Idaho is similar in its attitude to that of eastern Washington. Idaho and western Montana reflect a rugged individualism that, to a certain extent, is probably based on their short past.

In summary, close relationships exist between the physical situation and economic circumstances as one would expect in a region as young as the Northwestern States. The extractive industries are of great importance within the region and the characteristic of a net exporter of the results of primary processing bears witness to the underdeveloped regional markets. Greater growth in secondary processing awaits larger domestic markets.

The wheels of industry turn on low-cost hydroelectric power, the backbone of which has been developed by federal projects for the public welfare.

The pattern of regional specialization that results from the strong extractive industry orientation can be taken as an index of the economic maturity of the area as well as a basis for the prognostication of its future. An attempt to assess this future will be made in the final chapter.

3 *Population—The Settlement Pattern*

Some Quantitative Aspects.

THE POPULATION patterns of the Pacific Northwest are a study in demographic extremes. On the one hand, a whole quarter of the state of Oregon has a population concentration of 10 people or less per square mile, while the city of Seattle registers 6,810 per square mile. The Portland-Vancouver metropolitan area contains more people than the entire state of Idaho. The 100,000 people who watch the Rose Bowl football game on New Years Day are equivalent to a full half of the population of western Montana.

Idaho has no urban places which qualify for the category of "Urbanized Area" with the Bureau of Census, whereas Oregon has two—Portland and Eugene. Washington has three: Seattle, Tacoma, and Spokane.

As can be seen by Figure 5, the greatest concentrations of people occur in the Willamette-Puget Lowlands. From all indications it appears as though this area is undergoing the internal coalescence of smaller population nodes that ultimately develops into megalopolis and wall-to-wall people. The Northwest is no exception to either the national trend of a flight to the suburbs and urban fringe development or increasing urbanization. In the ten-year period, 1950–1960, Idaho, Oregon, and Washington experienced 25, 34, and 29 percent increases respectively in their urban populations.[6] As of 1960,

[6] U.S. Department of the Interior, Bonneville Power Administration, *Pacific Northwest Economic Base Study For Power Markets—Population,* Portland, Oregon, 1966.

68 percent of Washington's population was urban, while Oregon and Idaho recorded 62 and 47 percent. By themselves, the foregoing numbers only tell a portion of the story of population in the Northwest. As a region, during the 1950–1960 decade, population increase lagged slightly behind the U.S. average, 17.4 percent to 18.5 percent. Beginning with the era of 1960 it appears that western migration to the Northwestern States as a major source of population increase is at an end. This will cause the region to be dependent on intraregional reproductive change for increased population for the first time in its evolution.

The 1920–1930 migration figure in Table 1 represents almost half of the total population increase for that entire period. The peak

TABLE 1

Total Net Migration to Washington, Oregon and Idaho (1920–1960)*

1920–1930—179,522
1930–1940—250,514
1940–1950—667,004
1950–1960— 58,164

* U.S. Department of Interior, Bonneville Power Administration, Pacific Northwest Economic Base Study for Power Markets, *Population*, 1966.

period of migration was of course the period from 1940–1950 encompassing the war years and settlement of Reclamation Irrigation Projects. The figure for 1950–1960 speaks for itself and is illustrative of the decline of immigration as a principal source of population growth. There is no question that this decline is an important aspect of future economic growth in the region and that it reflects a major change in the population patterns of the Northwest.

Looking further into the demographic patterns that are beginning to take shape, it is possible to discern some internal characteristics that are similar to national trends. For instance, during the period 1950–1960 just a little less than half of the counties within the region lost population and the great bulk of those county units were rural in character. The rural counties constituted the major source of internal migration movement within the Northwestern States. This 1950–1960 decade saw the urban population increase 29 percent while rural population had a less than 1 percent increase. The destination of the population streams (including those from the central cities themselves) was for the most part the urban fringe of the larger metropolitan centers. Seattle, Tacoma, Spokane, Portland, and Eugene accounted for the greatest portion of these suburban accretions. The fact that cities in the 5,000 to 25,000 class were the recipients of the major influx and those 5,000 and under reported the smallest gains is yet another example of the propensity for population benefits to accrue to the already established regional commerce centers. During the 1950–1960 period the extraordinary 125 percent increase of population in the urbanized areas was due primarily to this phenomenon of urban fringe expansion.

Another characteristic the Northwest shares with national trends is the relationship between rates of natural increase and socioeconomic locations. Both southern Idaho and northeastern Oregon are rural areas and share the characteristic of highest rates of natural increase. On the other hand, southwestern Washington and northwestern Oregon are predominantly urban in character and have the region's lowest rates of natural increase.

Some Qualitative Aspects. While the foregoing data are pertinent to the description of the population characteristics of the region and are therefore germane to this book, it remains for something to be made of them. What do these things mean in a *qualitative* population sense? What is the import of rural areas continuing to have the higher rate of natural increase, but extremely low rates of total population growth? Apparently it is a pattern of emigration. When coupled with the drastic reduction in interregional migration with Northwestern destinations, this aspect takes on even greater importance. The Northwest will apparently have to rely on its rural areas for population growth and development. This suggests two very pertinent questions. Will the rural population migration be sufficient in quantity and quality to meet the needs of the industrial labor force, and what will be the effect of this emigration on the rural areas themselves? In order to at least partially answer the last question another qualitative aspect of the population needs to be discussed, that is, the relation of the non-working age group (18 and under, 65 and over) to the working age group.[7] A common method of expressing this relationship is the *dependency ratio,* which is a calculation based on the number of people in the non-working age group per 100 persons in the working group (18 to 65). As would probably be expected, the dependency ratio is highest in the rural regions and lowest in the urban areas. The predominantly rural areas of southern Idaho, for example, have a dependency ratio of 98. While it may seem redundant it is worthwhile to repeat here that this means that for every 100 persons of working age there are 98 individuals of dependent age in this area. The dependency ratio in western Washington, which is predominantly urban, is 82.

The impact of this situation on rural communities is staggering. The rural to urban migration is made up principally of working age people which depletes the labor force of the areas departed, causing a greater burden on those remaining. As will be noted in Table 2, the age group 24–44 has the highest participation rate in the labor force. This is exactly the age group category which is most mobile and makes up the bulk of the emigration from the rural areas previously mentioned.

The higher reproductive rate of the rural area continues to add to the non-working age group as does increased longevity resulting from longer life spans. The burden of school support along with other public and social programs clearly rests on a disproportionately smaller number of people of the working age when compared with the urban areas of the Northwest or of the nation as a whole.

For the whole region, the dependency ratio is highest in the rural

[7] This discussion draws heavily on Volume 2, part 2, *Labor Force.* Pacific Northwest Economic Base Study for Power Markets, Bonneville Power Administration, U.S. Department of Interior, 1966.

TABLE 2

*Age Composition and Participation Rates of the Male Labor Force,
Pacific Northwest.**

Age group	Percent of total group	Partcipation rate (percent of age group participating in labor force)
14–17	9.36	31.77
18–24	12.01	81.05
25–34	16.82	96.06
35–44	18.92	96.16
45–64	29.27	89.76
65 over	13.62	28.64

* U.S. Department of Interior, Bonneville Power Administration, Pacific Northwest Economic Base Study for Power Markets, *Labor Force*, 1966.

areas, which are also the areas that have the lowest per capita income. (See Figure 6.) These are the same regions that have net losses in their populations resulting from high emigration rates. It would seem that all of the interrelated ingredients are present for the fairly rapid development of rural deprivation.

There is not much doubt that we have not found the answer to the question, "How are you going to keep them down on the farm?" It is equally apparent that for the Northwest, at least, keeping them on the farm would only effectively reduce the labor force needed in commerce and industry located in the urban regions. The Marxist scheme of moving industry to the countryside is not only esthetically appalling but highly uneconomic (and, needless to say, politically undesirable). If the trend of western migration and settlement is broken, what are the answers to the continued need for labor force growth and the problems of the rural exodus that are posed here?

The "baby boom" that occurred in the decade 1940–1950 probably will provide a labor force cushion as it expands the number of working age people, but this apparent solution is a double-edged sword. If forecasts are correct, the expansion in the working age group will be greater in the next two decades than the present one. If employment opportunities are not spurred on by economic expansion, a situation conducive to regional emigration could occur (as well as higher unemployment).

To sum up, a rural decline is apparently inevitable. If employment opportunities keep pace with the expanding regional working age group, a rural to urban migration will continue, and if internal economic growth is insufficient, the migration will simply shift its direction outwardly to regions such as California. There seems to be no promise that the dependency ratios of the rural, low income areas will improve.

Country communities which have already passed over the threshold of rural retirement are already common in the Northwest. As economic *rigor mortis* sets in, the age distribution of its inhabitants is weighted heavily at the older end of the scale. Population declines, and stores and schools close. Consolidation with adjacent school districts continues to provide an education for the children, but it is no longer "their" school, and the old building becomes the community tombstone. As the tax base shrinks, public officials' and teachers' pay remains static. This is usually accompanied by their departure and a subsequent decline in the quality of services performed. It is no wonder that in these places there seems to be a greater orientation to the good old days of the past than to the present. It is not so surprising either that these are the places which respond so enthusiastically to those politicians who extoll the virtues of the past and urge a return to the ways of our fathers as salvation from the social, economic, and moral tribulations of the present. From their perspective on history, the past was clearly better than the present.

Other Qualitative Aspects. Despite the fact that the front wave of the frontier has passed the Northwest, some aspects of frontierism are still discernible.

The people of the Northwestern States have not yet shared equally in the trauma of the social revolution that is presently plaguing the nation. With the exception of the Indians and an episode or two dealing with the Chinese in its early history, the region has not yet experienced the social strife associated with minority groups in the American East and South. The region has been spared this humiliation primarily because of its youth, however, rather than for its possession of any human quality of understanding or mystical "western ethic" that prevails here, but not elsewhere in the republic.

Nothing much has happened to threaten the naturalistic freedom of the Northwesterner. His western hospitality is supposed to be something like southern hospitality with certain embellishments that make it better. While southern hospitality seems to have been directed at solidifying friendly relations within similar classes of people, western hospitality seems to be based on an expectation of mutual goodwill across, into, and through both class and color lines. The tests of the expectations which emanate from such an attitude, whether real or imagined, have yet to come because, for the most part, Northwesterners have not suffered from the tyranny of space socially. "Live and let live" is a social philosophy that is easily adopted where there is sufficient elbow room.

It may be fair to say that the Northwesterner is oblivious to intolerance insofar as ethnic or colored groups are concerned simply because minority groups are such a small proportion of the total population. In all of Washington, Oregon, Idaho, and Montana there are only 70,000 Blacks and 55,500 Indians (the next largest group).

Table 3 illustrates the distribution and change in the Negro population and is indicative of the national trend of migration to the more urbanized areas. Although the table does not show it directly, it does allude to the fact that rural settlement schemes, such as Bureau of Reclamation Irrigation Projects, have never been important to the Negro migratory facts of life. The Negro people's migration to the North has been urban oriented—away from the South and away from the farm and rural slums. The western agricultural open spaces, seemingly well suited to deliver the promise of

TABLE 3

*Negro Population in Northwestern States**

	1940	1960	Percent of all (1960)
Washington	7,424	48,738	1.7
Oregon	2,565	18,133	1.0
Idaho	595	1,502	.2
Montana	1,120	1,467	.2

* U.S. Department of Commerce, Statistical Abstract of United States, 1966.

a new start, stand out strikingly as being a means to a better life for families of those other than the Negro people.

The Northwesterners dare not remain complacent to the social unrest marked by the Black peoples' fair claim to equality under the Constitution. The small numbers represented by the Negro population statistics only serve to magnify the contrast between what is and what should be. In a free-swinging, supposedly socially unfettered western environment, *de facto* segregation and racial bias stand out as even greater incongruities. The urban places of Seattle, Tacoma, Portland, Vancouver, Spokane, and Pasco all have inner Negro communities that stand as mute testimony to the lack of any real differences in racial attitudes between the people of the Far West and the other segments of our country.

Controls of Population Distribution. It has been said at various times that in considering population distributions as much attention should be paid to where people are not as to where they are. In the Northwest, as in other places of the world, population concentrations are least in areas of geographic extremes. But in the Northwest there is an additional system of population distribution that deserves our attention because of the unique aspects of its existence and its effect qualitatively on the people concerned. What is being referred to is the planned, administratively-decreed distribution of Indians and their lands. None of the dynamic factors of location were operative in the situation of the reservation lands. As a result, the system of population distribution that emerges is an entirely artificial one inasmuch as there has been little freedom for individuals to respond to the multitude of factors which influence the choice of location of other peoples.

This is not to say that the Indian people are not free to come and go as they please or to take advantage of special relocation services and sever relations with the tribe and reservation entirely, if they so desire. But the fact remains that economic circumstances and a reluctance to substitute the uncertainty of a new place and unfamiliar people for the certainty of their home environment has had a dampening effect on migration. There are thirty-one Indian reservations in the Northwestern region and characteristically about half of the Indians on the tribal rolls still reside on their respective reservations.

The effects of forced settlement by establishing reservations for Indian people have been difficult to cope with. In setting them apart (most frequently on marginal lands), integration has been made more difficult. Situating reservations in rural, undeveloped economic environments has detracted from the extent and quality of the education process. Services normally available to the suburban dweller on a "walk-in" basis are restricted to a bare minimum if they exist at all. Working for wages is generally confined to farm labor in adjacent areas. Commuting to jobs in nearby towns is practically unheard of. The yearly average family income for reservation Indians is approximately $2000. This varies from a low of $390 to a high approaching $5000.[8] It should be mentioned that for the most part the higher incomes are usually associated with the settlement of some claim pertaining to land ownership or fishing rights so that these incomes do not reflect the productivity per se of either the Indians or their land.

The dropout rate after grade 8 in the Indian schools is very high. Consequently the educational achievement levels are depressed. For

[8] U.S. Department of Interior, Bureau of Indian Affairs, *Indian Reservations of the Northwest* (Portland, Oregon, 1960).

the age group 21 to 30, the average achievement is the ninth grade. For the 30 to 50 group it is grade 6, and over age 50 it is grade 3. As a rule the younger generations are better educated, but the educational needs are still greater than the accomplishments. A common, recurring statement of need on practically all reservations is an adequate, clean water supply and proper waste disposal systems.

The self-determination principle and subsequent liquidation of Indian lands is a process which is beginning to gain momentum. The Klamath Indian Reservation in southern Oregon is an example of such a program, but it was somewhat unique in that the tribal lands contained forest lands of considerable value. Those inhabitants who did not wish to participate in the dissolution of the reservation were accorded allotments of land within the former reservation, while the bulk of the property was sold.

The economic and social stagnation so characteristic of reservation Indian families is the consequence of impaired mobility produced by the static location of the tribal grounds. The Indian was deprived of choosing his territorial base at the outset by the establishment of reservations that propagated both social and economic characteristics unable to cope with the rapid changes that occur in the predominant "outside" cultural environment.

CITY AND TOWN TYPES

A second important part of the settlement pattern of the region is the nature of its cities and towns from the point of view of their functional existence. The author is well aware of the multifunctional aspects of cities and the ensuing problems generated by the introduction of a classification. Needless to say, most systems of categorization must choose to ignore certain things and the following discussion will be no exception.

The chosen categories present the idea that while there may be no unique places (functionally speaking) in this region, the patterns that result from viewing the cities through this classificatory device will help to reveal part of the character of the region. The classification is neither unique nor exhaustive, and no attempt has been made to provide a "fit" for each town and village of the region.

Because of the relative youth of the region, changes in the functions of urban places have been minimal and restricted in scope. As would be expected, the most favored locations have produced the most dynamic cities. For the most part, these places are those whose hinterlands have provided growth through enlarging their areas or by intensified economic activity.

Resource Oriented. The most prominent feature of the urban pattern of the Northwestern States is the large number of its cities which are predominantly resource oriented in their functional character. Almost half of the cities with populations over 2500 are in this category with agriculture as the most important and prevalent hinterland activity. Forestry and mining provide the remainder of the resource oriented cities with their *raison d'être*. Examples of cities that are typical of this category are: Yakima, Washington, (agriculture); Lewiston, Idaho (forestry); and Wallace-Kellogg, Idaho (mining).

Commerce and Manufacturing. A very small number of cities, restricted to the largest in size, owe their present functional existence to large-scale trade operations or manufacturing activity. The Seattle-Tacoma and Portland-Vancouver areas easily surpass all other nodal regions in this respect. These areas are responsible for such activities as aircraft manufacture, shipbuilding, furniture making, small-scale steel making and iron foundries, fabrication of sports clothing, recreational boat building, and equipment and machinery of a great variety.

The ports of Seattle, Tacoma, and Portland are important terminals for internal shipping along the Columbia portal, gathering points for outbound commodities by both ship and rail, and for inbound freight from the Orient and California. The multifunctional aspects of these cities is largely the result of the generalized growth factors previously mentioned. As the most favored locations, the scope of activities of these areas is bound to increase in the future.

Transportation Centers. There are obvious relations between commerce and transportation which will make differentiation a somewhat subjective operation. There are, however, some cities in the Northwest whose predominant orientation is toward the function of transportation and transport facilities and in which commerce is not emphasized per se. For the sake of simplicity three categories of transport sub-functions—gateway (internal and external), junction, and terminus—may be identified as special services provided by the unique locations of some Northwestern transport centers. The two aspects of the gateway transport center recognize the importance of both inbound and outbound traffic. Spokane, Washington, and Pocatello, Idaho, are examples of mountain gateway cities important to inbound transportation lines. Portland, Oregon, is probably the most important external transport center for it sits at the head of the internal water transport system of the Columbia River and two of the important national rail systems. As previously mentioned, it is the major Northwestern seaport.

Pasco, Washington, with one of the largest automated gravity switching railroad yards in the United States, is the outstanding example of the junction sub-function of transportation centers. A "railroad town" since its beginning, this city has prospered by its strategic location on a low level route from the coast inland along the Columbia River. The junction aspect of its location will be enhanced further as inland water transportation is extended further up the Snake River.

The terminus sub-function can be characterized by the port cities having facilities to handle inbound crude petroleum and outbound refined products. While this may be slightly unconventional in terms of classification, the ports of Anacortes and Ferndale on Puget Sound in Washington do represent the terminus of a crude oil pipeline originating in Canada. The tidewater locations of the installations include deep water handling facilities so that in the future crude petroleum from Alaska as well as foreign areas can be terminated and refined at these locations.

Educational and Institutional. Educational centers abound in the Northwest and perhaps as a category are one of the most discernible. The educational function is clearly predominant in such places as Corvallis (Oregon), Bozeman (Montana), and Pullman (Washington). Surrounded by the great wheat producing region of the Palouse, Washington State University, a land grant college grown into university, is without a doubt the prime source from which Pullman derives its life. Other institutional services provided by the states serve as foundations for community growth and development. Mental hospitals, penal institutions, and large branches of federal bureaus all share in this role, as do political centers such as state capitals.

Special Service. Special service functions are performed in a variety of classes by Northwest cities. Some of the outstanding categories are recreation and tourism, operation and maintenance, and mobile labor centers or "boom towns."

Recreation and tourist oriented communities include Sun Valley, Idaho; Seaside, Oregon; and Pacific Beach, Washington. Operation and maintenance centers such as Coulee Dam (Washington), Bonneville (Oregon), and Nespelem (Washington) serve as the loci for an agglomeration of people engaged in the overseeing and manipulation of federally constructed dams in the first two instances and the operation of the Colville Indian Reservation in the latter case.

Mobile labor centers or "boom towns" are quite singular in their function. In the Northwestern States the most frequent circumstance conducive to their establishment is related to dam building. The construction involved in the addition of a third powerhouse at Grand Coulee Dam will no doubt cause a re-creation in part, at least, of the original merchants' paradise that was Coulee Dam during the construction period of the late 1930s.

Combinations. Modification of initial functions leading to a broader scope of services or multiple service roles engendered by unique locations are largely responsible for the cities which belong to the category of *combination*. For instance, while Spokane, Washington, is an important mountain gateway city into the region, it is also affected by its juxtaposition with a large and prosperous agricultural hinterland dominated by a wheat monoculture. The special accessibility rendered by the transportation lines which focus on Spokane offer special advantages for distribution to a large "inland empire" that it has dominated as the central city for some time. Industry in modest proportions related to the building trades and special fabrication catering to the expanding markets especially peculiar to the region such as mobile homes, transportation equipment, and boat building, are providing for much more diversification in the service functions of this city.

Other cities which combine a fewer number of factors than those pertinent to Spokane are Missoula, Montana, and Eugene, Oregon, which combine the resource oriented function of forestry with that of education, and Boise, Idaho, which blends agriculture with its institutional role as the state capital.

In the beginning of this section, it was stated that those places which had undergone the most change in their service functions over time were the most favored, and in what might be termed a constructive sense, this is true. There are some places, however, that have been least favored and have incurred as much change in what could be called a destructive sense. For example, numerous places have been plunged into decline and even non-existence by radical changes in natural resource availability, modifications in the structural nature of agriculture, decreased accessibility resulting from alteration of the transportation network, or decline in the importance of a particular mode of transportation.

The townsites of Murray, Pritchard, and Concord in Idaho, for example, have undergone the change brought on by mineral depletion. The twenty-year period from 1860–1880 in Idaho saw numerous gold camps come and go as placer deposits were quickly worked out. Concord, in the Buffalo Hump country, is one town that has gone. All that remains of the original townsite are a few utility poles and bottle heaps in an alpine meadow. Murray and Pritchard were important sites in the Coeur d'Alene gold rush that occurred in the 1880s. These two places still exist, but their dependence has shifted to logging and a little hard rock mining. While their populations in the 1880s were measured in the thousands, now they are in the hundreds.

Springdale, Washington is one of those places that has suffered a decline as a result of major structural changes in agriculture. Founded in 1889 when the Spokane Falls and Northern Railroad provided access from Spokane to southern Stevens County, this site was an important producer of timothy hay for the horse feed markets in Spokane. When horses were replaced by mechanical power in the ensuing twenty years, a mainstay of the economy of Springdale was displaced. Logging and mining were also active adjacent to the town and managed to extend its life somewhat.

In general, larger farms have led to fewer farmsteads and declining populations in the smaller service centers in the region. These small towns had fewer job opportunities and lacked the amenities of the next larger service center in the hierarchy. Hierarchal leap-frogging resulted and economically stranded some of the smallest agricultural towns. When they become bypassed by the newest transportation grids whose purpose is to link the service centers of the present, their dereliction will be complete.

In more recent times, Byron and Starbuck, Washington, felt the impact of an alteration of the transportation network. Byron, a small community in the Yakima Valley, was bypassed and entered the phase of decline when the main valley highway was relocated. Starbuck was a railroad roundhouse location on the Oregon-Washington Railroad and Navigation Company line. It met its economic downfall when the roundhouse facilities were relocated as a part of a consolidation with another larger rail line. With the advent of bulk hauling by motor freight, many small Northwestern towns that were on the local "milk run" train schedules were subsequently by-passed by the rail line in order to compete more readily with this new form of transportation.

Cascade Locks, located on the Washington side of the lower Columbia River, is another site that went into a depressed state of development as the result of the decline in the importance of a mode of transport. The town was located at the head of a mechanical portage system around the falls and rapids occurring in the Columbia in the immediate vicinity. Cargo was both loaded and unloaded at this point, and when slack water navigation was brought to the lower Columbia by Bonneville Dam, the economic damage had been done. Larger boats and barges could be used after the dam was built and the importance of Cascade Locks was then a matter of history.

SOME INTERESTING SETTLEMENT PATTERNS

Urban sprawl, preplanned cities, and an agricultural area display-ing unusual regularity in its town spacing provide the student of the Pacific Northwest with some interesting cultural phenomena.

Spreading out from the major urban centers of the Pacific coast, people have created an effect much akin to a dye stain as they permeate the fabric of the landscape and run out along the arteries which can absorb them most readily. The confining physical features of areas adjacent to the Willamette-Puget Trough restrict the out-ward fling of population movement to some extent and the natural economic attraction of the city centers themselves has resulted in a growth pattern whose major directional component is north-south. The area from Everett, Washington, on the north to Tacoma on the south represents the only tendency for a conurbation in the region. The state capital of Olympia will no doubt join this expanding nucleus soon and even a few of the more optimistic prognosticators envision a megalopolis extending from Portland, Oregon, to Everett, Washington.

The elopement of the middle class with the urban fringe areas has supplied the momentum for the population sprawl here as elsewhere, although expanding and new industries attracted to the coastal region have also played important parts in the filling in of the interstices of the pre-war settlement pattern. As has been the case with other regions, this urban flight has created a variety of problems for the central business districts as the entrepreneurs follow their market and create new and attractive shopping centers immediately accessible to their automotive oriented suburban buyers. The lament of those businessmen unwilling or unable to relocate is like that of the merchants who saw their cities surpassed by some others in the process of economic maturing. A typical comment from this region was something like, "The only trouble with Tacoma is Seattle."

The unincorporated bedroom communities of the Northwest are just like their counterparts in any other location in the United States with the exception perhaps that its environs may be more scenic and in some cases more roomy. They represent the most rapidly expanding segments of the region and characteristically are made up of the middle and upper middle class whites. Taxes tend to be higher than state averages but such things as school support are unquestioned and the school systems that result are impressive educationally as well as architecturally.

To a certain extent, urban sprawl in the region has been looked on as a blight upon the land. It would be unrealistic to apply the strict environmental preservation requirements of the National Park Service to the urban fringe housing developments and yet to satisfy the ethic of the Northwesterner something of this nature seems desirable. Where a real estate developer gives birth to a new tract of land, the bulldozer is apt to be turned loose on the landscape indiscriminately, but husbands and wives are just as likely to tie yarn and string around trees and rocks they wish their contractor to save, causing him no end of inconvenience in the process. The implication is clear: equipment is to be manipulated, the landscape is not.

From another aspect of blight, suburban sprawl seems directly responsible for the creation of urban housing vacuums. As areas become stranded, landlords disregard their former tenant restrictions, and minority segments of the population, particularly Negroes, are allowed to assume tenancy. This of course has the undesirable effect of continued separatism, its location just changes. Temporarily both parties are assuaged, but only temporarily. The Negro family knows that their "new" location has been made possible only by the dispersion of the former white tenants and the desire of the landlord to maintain his income. Invariably, these locations are in the older portions of Northwest cities and it should have been far more obvious than it seems to have been, that a "used" white neighborhood and a sub-standard one at that, would serve only to sharpen the contrasts of our supposedly equalitarian society. The population movement to the suburbs is bound to continue in the Pacific Northwest and the propagation of these undesirable effects will naturally follow unless freedom of movement and settlement become realities for all of the people of the region.

The complications produced by the rapid population surge to the suburbs were more than could be coped with by the local governments. While urban planning enjoyed something of a history in the Puget Sound area, the guidelines for intra-urban or regional planning caused by urban fringe developments were non-existent. As a result, Seattle's lovely Lake Washington became a gigantic open air cesspool; watershed management had to be increased; larger and more automobile arterials had to be planned and their construction expedited. Fortunately, local regional planning was initiated and took place as rapidly as the political process would allow it. Pollution control measures reversed the trend toward a decline in the environmental quality. Lake Washington has been rejuvenated and is now open again for public swimming and recreation, and the rapid pollution of Puget Sound has been cut back drastically. In what appears in planning to be the inevitable interim between recognition of a problem caused by progress and the beginning of its solution, however, sufficient time elapsed to allow the development of land uses which are not in keeping with the major thrust of environmental quality control or even public safety. The commercial strand developments that mushroom up alongside the super highways between the urban centers of Seattle and Tacoma are prime examples. Despite all of our protective attitudes the urban Northwesterner is being plagued by an excess of the problems created by a suburban automotive society.

Preplanned Cities. Two cities in Washington have the distinction of being the only preplanned communities in the Pacific Northwest. Longview, a forest industry oriented town along the Columbia River, was the first city in the region to have been planned in its entirety and built on a site which was converted from farm and woodland to a predetermined urban shape.

Around 1918, the Long-Bell Lumber Company became interested in the Northwest as a place to renew their declining economic vigor that had been based on the southern pine region. Largely through the efforts of Mr. Long, who was determined that the human and capital resources accumulated by the company would neither go to waste nor be used to develop just another big lumber camp, the idea of the city of Longview was committed to paper on the drafting boards.

Zoning of Longview was accomplished through restrictions placed on the use of the various parcels of land by the company. Six classes of land use were recognized and juxtaposed in the plan quite in keeping with contemporary concepts. Residential, apartment, central retail, outlying retail, light industrial and heavy industrial constituted the major categories of land use. A civic center which included a theater, library, churches, and other public buildings was planned in a somewhat traditional New England style including a central park. Roads, sidewalks, and curbs were all paved with concrete even where there were no buildings. Vacant lots were landscaped, giving the impression in the early days of a huge estate with very formal English gardens.

The town was founded in 1923 and quickly grew to a population of 10,000 people. The original site was overplanned for there are still streets and vacant lots which await their settlement and use.

The present city of Richland, Washington, had some of the elements of the preplanning of Longview, but in this case a small hamlet by that name already existed. It became the city it is now by architectural design, however, including the distribution system of a variety of housing types when the nearby site of Hanford was chosen by the United States Government as the place for the reactors that were to supply the nation with nuclear energy.

There were about 240 residents in the area of Richland in 1943 when the government program of land acquisition was begun. The small irrigated farms and wasteland were converted into a city according to a preconceived plan. The duPont and General Electric Companies were its primary benefactors and source of governance until after the end of the Second World War. The population is now approximately 25,000, and while many of the smaller prefabricated houses have been removed, the larger homes remain as do the main buildings in the shopping center.

Both of these cities may be termed boom towns or company towns for that matter, but hardly in the traditional sense. Even in the unoccupied areas within the town bounds, the planned use approach is responsible for a welcome change from the chaotic growth of towns which had the same impetus for expansion but were without the essential ingredient of reasoned foresight.

Town Spacing in the Dryland Wheat Area. In southeastern Washington where a dry land wheat monoculture prevails, the relationships existing between the predominant land use and its urban service centers provides an interesting example of urban-rural interaction. Fifty percent of the towns that are clearly functionally oriented toward service to this dry land wheat area are between 20 and 26 miles apart. The average for the entire group is 21 miles. (In a smaller sub-group on the north and eastern margin of the Palouse region where ownership parcels are smaller, the towns average a distance of 9 miles apart.)

The farms are immense and farmsteads tend to be widely spaced. The juxtaposition of farm after farm and the similarity of the farmers' response to the matrix of economic and geographic production factors of the region would naturally tend to create a spatial system that would display characteristics of regularity in the spacing of towns functionally oriented toward the wheat monoculture of the area. Similarity in the mode of transport and equivalence in access to the transportation network are also important factors in the town pattern. In this region, those towns which are served both by road and rail are larger in population, and there is a tendency for some regularity in the spacing of these larger centers. In short, a miniature hierarchy of agricultural service centers seems to exist in this area and invites further study.

4 *Water and Regional Economic Development*

I̲ᴛ ʜᴀs been said that the West is not a place, but rather an idea. That idea probably emanates from the implied promise of this land and the willingness of its settlers to achieve a livelihood while maintaining an unusual sense of compatibility with the environment.

The planned use of the Pacific Northwest's surface water endowment is an outstanding example of the fruition of the western idea. The utilization of water for purposes of creating hydroelectric power and providing irrigation water constitutes the most important resource development of the region.

Inherent in the structure of the plans for development of the region's water resources, however, was an assumption that water, like the air and minerals found in the public domain, was free. For some reason it did not occur to the state governments that a fee for the appropriation of water could serve both as a source of revenue and as a means of regulating or allocating scarce resources.

This concept of free water has tended to insulate water development projects from the economic scrutiny that would otherwise occur and has been responsible for taking a longer time than necessary to ascertain the value of water in its alternative uses. As a consequence, Northwestern economic growth associated with water resource development has not always profited from the review that ensues with the observation that a resource is becoming more scarce and therefore more valuable.

A predisposition for development practices of the past is a luxury the region can no longer afford as the notion of competing uses for water based on its value begins to include regional competition, as has occurred between California, Arizona, and other Southwestern States.

HYDRO-POWER DEVELOPMENT

Due to the scarcity of fossil fuels within the region and the almost universal availability of streams convertible to electrical energy production, hydroelectricity provides over 90 percent of the electrical energy requirements of the region. Washington is the leading water power state of the area, followed by Idaho, Oregon, and Montana.

The northwestern streams have not been ready-made for the use of man. Their cyclical flows must be evened out in order for electricity to be available during all periods of the year. Adjustments must also be made to accommodate the regional differences in the timing of peak flows of the streams. West of the Cascades, maximum streamflow periods occur during the winter months (with few exceptions), while on the east, peak periods occur during the summer months. Eastern streamflows offer by far the greatest electrical potential. The demand, however, for power is greatest on the west. In terms of the "constancy requirement" for electricity, the scheme for development was clear—it would be necessary to integrate the power systems of both sides of the mountains and, in so doing, create storage and transmission facilities that would complement each other.

The Basin Concept. Out of these necessities came the ideas of the basin concept and multiple use that are development measures of both the Corps of Engineers and the Bureau of Reclamation. The basin concept of water resource planning is the natural outgrowth of what could be called a holistic approach so common to the tradition of geography. Delineating the entire drainage basin of the Columbia River system and adapting a developmental program which recognizes the uniqueness of certain sites and the necessity for an integrated network of all of them to attain maximum development of the resource potential are basic to the basin development concept.

By far the greatest concern in this type of water development is the building of upstream dams and reservoirs whose manipulation can provide a constant flow of water throughout all seasons. The more dams that can be placed downstream of the storage control fixtures, the more electricity can be generated from the same water. Adequate flood control for the drainage system is an integral part of this planning. Grand Coulee Dam and its reservoir, Roosevelt Lake, provide this necessary Columbia River flow regulation for nine existing downstream dams. These nine run-of-the-river dams have no storage features themselves, despite the fact that large lakes are impounded by them. These lakes serve the purpose of providing a "head" for each dam—that is, a distance for the water to fall and thereby turn the turbine-generator complex that creates the electrical power. Other key basin storage projects are Hells Canyon, Brownlee, and Oxbow on the middle Snake River; Hungry Horse on the Flathead; Libby Dam now under construction on the Kootenai; and Duncan, Arrow Lake, and Mica Creek dams in British Columbia on the uppermost Columbia. These new Canadian dams are now under construction and represent the latest and most necessary projects needed to fulfill the requirements of the basin concept on the Columbia River. Duncan and Arrows dams are unique in that they are designed as storage projects without any facilities for generation of at-site power.

The Columbia, Snake, Willamette, Kootenai, Pend Oreille, and Skagit rivers account for the largest share of the regional runoff. Of these six streams, only two, the Willamette and Skagit, are located west of the Cascades. While the Skagit is well suited to hydroelectric development, the Willamette is not. The Skagit River is the only one of this group that is not a tributary of the Columbia, which is illustrative of the predominance of the Columbia system and of the necessity for a scheme that integrates regional water resources to provide optimum development of the basin concept.

The Columbia provides 60 percent of the regional runoff at its mouth, but of course this includes the enhancement of all of its tributaries. This stream has the greatest hydroelectric potential even though its fall is exceeded by others.

The region is ideally suited to hydroelectric development inasmuch as its streams are relatively free of particles in suspension, dam sites that fulfill the physical requirements are numerous, and much space, often in the public domain, is available for reservoirs. On the negative side, however, is the fact that many of the potential dam sites constitute poor economic locations since they are far from regional load centers. This circumstance offers still another reason for an integrated, interconnected regional electrical system.

One more thing should be said of the progress associated with the basin concept. The element conspicuous by its absence has been an economic evaluation of dam sites that would lead to a sequential order of development and thus optimum capital allocation. The drainage basin of the Columbia includes parts of four sovereign states and one foreign country, and the full development of all parts of the basin has not always been uppermost in the minds of the men chosen to engage in the political processes necessary for interstate agreements and enabling legislation.

Multiple Use. The multiple use idea of water resource development is not as broad a concept as basin development but rather serves as a guideline for the measurement of the diversity of individual projects. Hydroelectric power, irrigation, recreation, navigation, and flood control are the most prominent of these multiple uses, and collectively they pose the question: Is this site being developed with thought being given to the variety of uses of the water?

While the idea of serving as many masters as possible is appealing, it almost constitutes an ironclad guarantee that no single use, irrespective of its importance, will be developed to its maximum potential. Certain natural conflicts are easily suggested. For the most efficient hydroelectric operation, all water should pass through the turbines without a drop being used for other purposes. If, however, a dam blocks the migration of anadromous fish, some water must be used for fish passage facilities. For maximum flood control, up-stream reservoir sites should be drawn down preceding expected peak flows. This might leave recreational facilities high and dry, while also creating greater pumping distances if irrigation water is involved. In short, while the roots of the multiple purpose concept are in conservation and the idea of deriving as much good from a project as possible, it must be recognized that this scheme inherently causes a foregoing of additional benefits that may accrue as the result of a plan that is more singular in its scope, but chooses to emphasize the most profitable aspect of its situation.

Allocation of costs associated with the multipurpose federal projects as reflected by their repayment schedules offers a simple means of discussing this particular aspect of water resource development. Bonneville Dam is a run-of-the-river structure and as such has no storage facilities, therefore, it cannot claim to serve the purpose of flood control. Neither is it able to charge off part of its cost to irrigation. However, it creates electricity, provides for inland navigation, enhances recreation possibilities, and contains a fish ladder. Of these last four uses, only one is a direct source of revenue—electricity. While the locks and lake make inland navigation possible and these are a benefit to society in general, their costs are essentially non-reimbursable. The same is true for recreation and fish passage facilities. It can be seen in this instance that revenue from the electrical plant must be the principal source for repayment of the costs of construction. In contrast, Coulee Dam serves every one of the multiple uses except fish passage. It too has some non-reimbursable phases, however, as there are no immediate assignees for the flood control benefits or improvement of inland navigation. Hydroelectricity and irrigation are the principal revenue sources associated with this dam. The extent of the non-reimbursable portions of all northwestern federal water resource projects serves the purpose of illustrating the nature of the capital requirements of these public works projects and their importance to the economic development of the region.

It should be noted here that the benefits which accrue to a multiple use dominated scheme are increased to a great extent by the establishment of river regulation through large storage projects. The more water that is controlled, the greater is the flexibility of downstream uses and this one issue is at the very heart of what has been a long and acrimonious battle between the public and private power entities in the Northwestern hydroelectric development field. By their very nature, storage projects capable of manipulating large quantities of water are expensive, either because of the size of the undertaking or the sacrifice of at-site power production to water control. When a portion of these costs can be borne by the economic enhancement of downstream facilities as a basin concept of development presupposes, the costs can be borne by the entire system. If, on the other hand, the scope of operations is reduced to something far less than an entire drainage basin the accounting problems rise almost exponentially. It should be fairly clear that the costs of dams that provide the essential storage, such as Grand Coulee, Hungry Horse, and the newer Canadian Treaty dams, are beyond the normal financial grasp of private power companies unless even greater concessions are made in the form of subsidies or the overlooking of the various aspects of monopoly.

Power Developers. The major developers of the surface waters for hydroelectric purposes fall generally into three main groups: public utility districts, private power corporations, and the federal agencies of the Bureau of Reclamation and Corps of Engineers. Other offices of national government have aided in the growth and distribution of the electrical energy, such as the Bonneville Power Administration and the Rural Electricification Administration. In recent years, both public and private utilities have combined to share in the construction of generating facilities, which is illustrative of a rare case of cooperation. The public vs. private power controversy has been going on for over twenty years in the Pacific Northwest, but of course is not by any means a phenomenon unique to this area. The private power companies of the Northwest, in concert with those of the rest of the United States, have sometimes intimated in the manner of a thinly veiled threat that public ownership of the electrical industry was a socialistic menace. When that idea became less acceptable, their educational materials stressed that public ownership was inherently anti-free enterprise which amounted to un-Americanism. Private power companies also decried the unfair advantage gained by public developers in low interest rates for capitalization requirements; the diversion of public funds for water development purposes rather than being utilized for such things as the space program; and the loss of taxes to local communities ordinarily paid by a private utility. Public power proponents, on the other hand, sketch the private power companies as being only tax collectors who pass these costs on to the consumer; point to the fast tax write-offs made possible by defense mobilization activities under which many private dams have been built as generous non-interest bearing subsidies; cite rural electrification as being at least partially accomplished by the lower interest rates; and claim that the early increase in farm productivity (to say nothing of comfort) made possible by the distribution of electricity to the rural areas more than compensates for the depressed interest rates. The higher consumer costs of private power electricity (see Figure 7) are pointed out as being related to the necessity for stock income, and when the arguments become particularly heated it is usually mentioned that a good number of the large stockholders of the private Northwest electrical industry reside elsewhere. It is probably fair to say that the major thrust of the public utilities argument is based on the advisability of developing public resources by means other than those which will assure a maximum of benefits with a minimum of cost and a distribution of those benefits for social as well as capital gain. In short, building by the people for the people. The private power companies, on the other hand, feel confident that the incentives supplied by free enterprise are sufficient for the development of an efficient electrical industry and that, to an extent, public utilities and certainly the national government represent unfair competition in the electrical business.

Fortunately, one developer does not have to prevail over the other in order for resource development to continue. The federal system of dams and the power grid that connects them provide the backbone for the electrical industry. The Bonneville Power Administration plays the leading role as both the disseminator of power generated by federally built facilities and as the integrator for all electrical generation in the region. The Northwest Power Pool, a voluntary organization of all agencies involved in power generation, was spearheaded by the Bonneville Power Administration. It has provided the leadership and transmission facilities for the interconnected distribution system from which all utilities benefit. Through this system, electricity from all utilities is transmitted to the load centers of the region, exchanges of power are made possible, and, most recently, a large market has become accessible through an intertie of transmission facilities with the Southwest. The operation of the "preference clause," which stipulates that preference will be given by the Bonneville Power Administration to public and other municipally or cooperatively owned electrical suppliers at times when there is insufficient power for all of its customers, is a constant reminder to the private power companies that it has an interest in keeping ahead of demand schedules and also in encouraging the federal generation system to do the same. In 1967, the private power companies of the Pacific Northwest supplied 23.5 percent of the total energy generated, while purchasing a little over $13 million worth of electricity from the Bonneville Power Administration, practically all of which was firm power.

The advent of the 1964 treaty with Canada made it necessary to formalize the 20-year-old voluntary Northwest Power Pool, and a new coordination agreement between the Bonneville Power Administration, Corps of Engineers, and fourteen other generating utilities has been consummated.

New Columbia River Developments.   The 1964 Canadian Water Development Treaty is the single most important part of the Columbia River basin development to occur. Under its provisions, three dams are to be built in British Columbia and one in the United

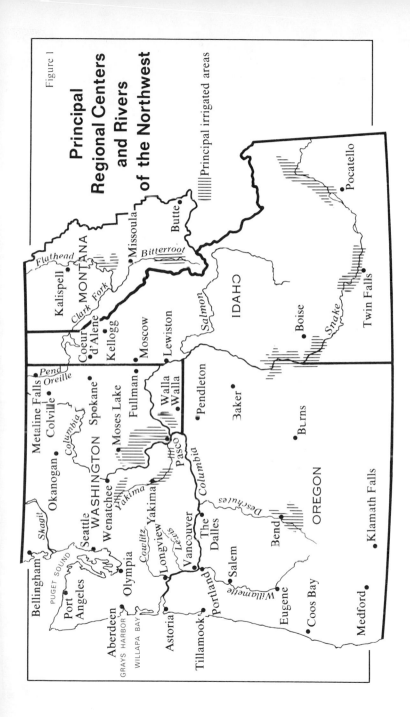

Figure 1

Principal Regional Centers and Rivers of the Northwest

Principal irrigated areas

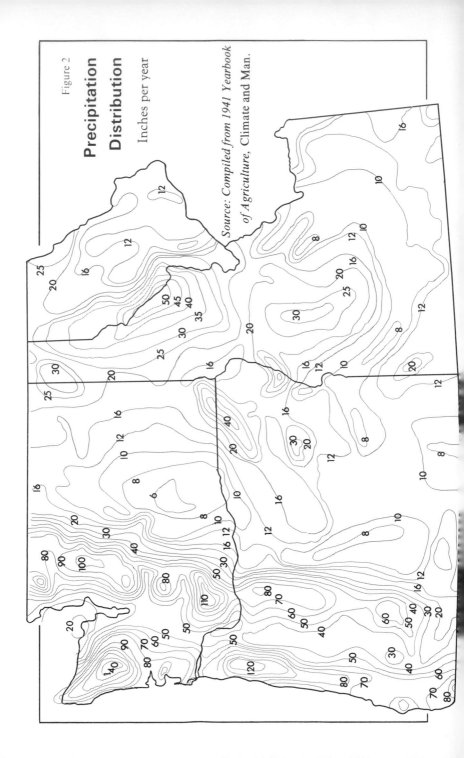

Figure 2

Precipitation Distribution

Inches per year

Source: Compiled from 1941 Yearbook of Agriculture, Climate and Man.

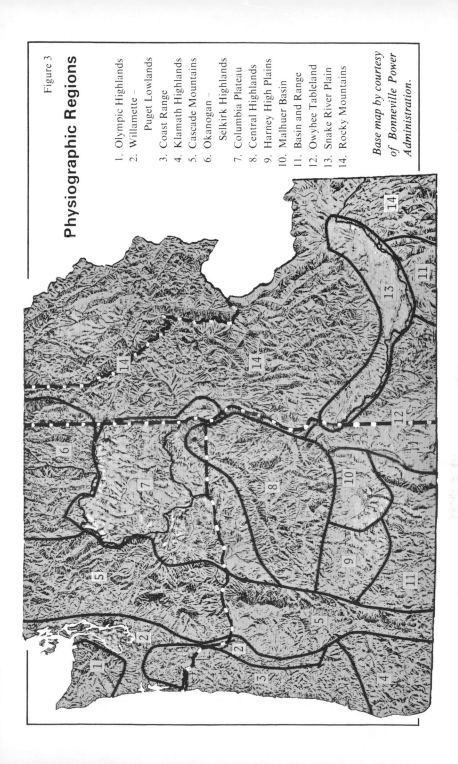

Figure 3

Physiographic Regions

1. Olympic Highlands
2. Willamette –
   Puget Lowlands
3. Coast Range
4. Klamath Highlands
5. Cascade Mountains
6. Okanogan –
   Selkirk Highlands
7. Columbia Plateau
8. Central Highlands
9. Harney High Plains
10. Malhuer Basin
11. Basin and Range
12. Owyhee Tableland
13. Snake River Plain
14. Rocky Mountains

Base map by courtesy of Bonneville Power Administration.

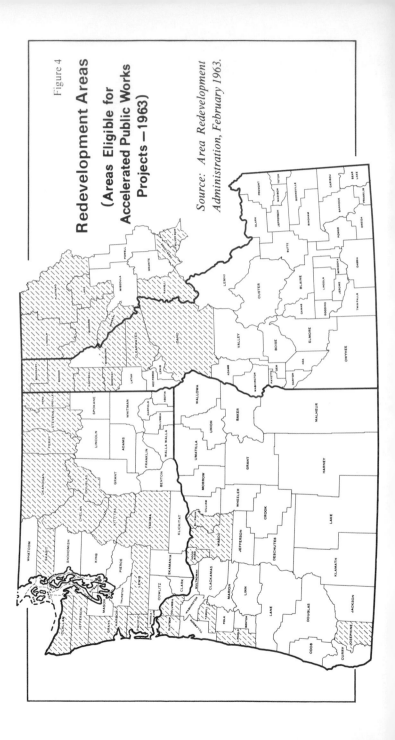

Figure 4

Redevelopment Areas

(Areas Eligible for Accelerated Public Works Projects — 1963)

Source: Area Redevelopment Administration, February 1963.

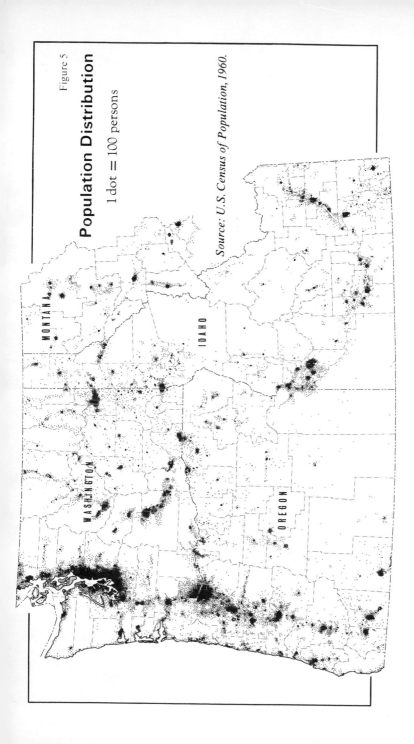

Figure 5

Population Distribution

1 dot = 100 persons

Source: U.S. Census of Population, 1960.

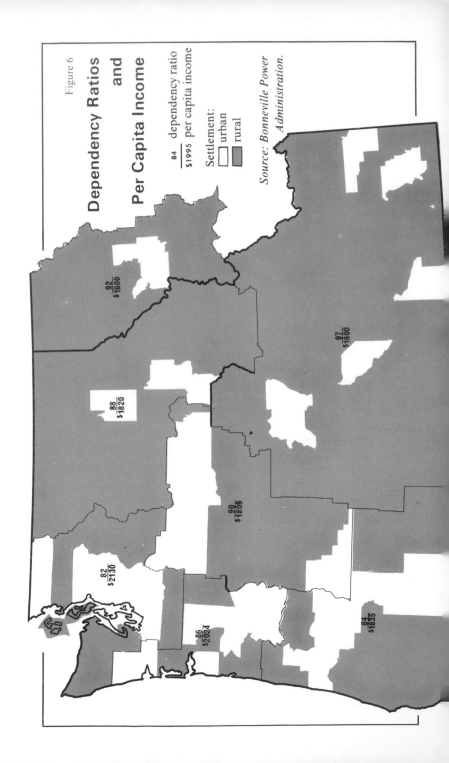

Figure 6

Dependency Ratios
and
Per Capita Income

84 dependency ratio
$1995 per capita income

Settlement:
☐ urban
▨ rural

Source: Bonneville Power
Administration.

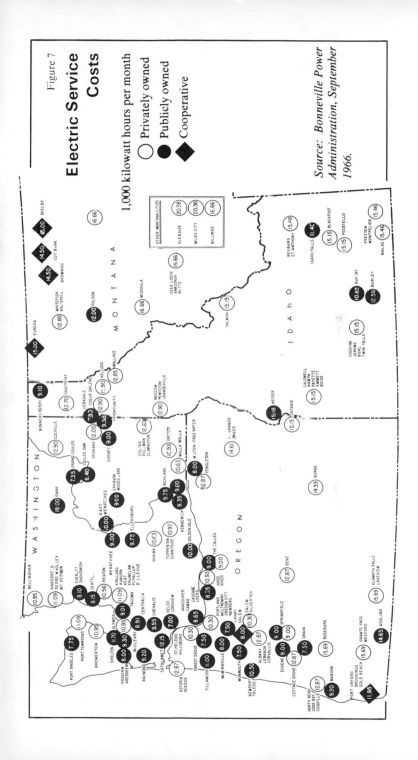

Figure 7

Electric Service
Costs

1,000 kilowatt hours per month

○ Privately owned

● Publicly owned

◆ Cooperative

*Source: Bonneville Power
Administration, September
1966.*

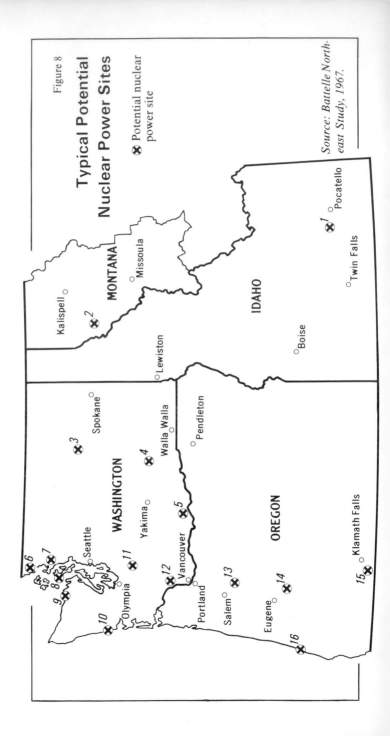

Figure 8

Typical Potential Nuclear Power Sites

⊗ Potential nuclear power site

Source: Battelle Northeast Study, 1967.

States, which would create 15½ million acre feet of upstream storage. This storage increase more than doubles the existing storage capabilities in the Northwestern States and will be of great significance in the control of floods and the increase of the power potential of downstream dams. This additional regulatory control of the flow of the Columbia will ultimately make it possible for these downstream dams to produce many additional kilowatts of firm power. A third powerhouse is already under construction at Grand Coulee Dam where an additional twelve turbines and generators will be housed to bring the total generating capacity from 2 to 9.2 million kilowatts. Chief Joseph, Rocky Reach, and The Dalles dams, all on the Columbia, will add eleven, four, and eight new turbines and generators respectively between the present and 1974.

In terms of flood control, when all the treaty dams are completed, the historic flood levels of 1894 and 1948 would be cut back to 24 feet at the lower end of the Columbia. The Northwest Public Power Association likes to point out that 24 feet is the level of the basement floor under their administration building in Vancouver, Washington. Flood control benefits accruing to the United States as a result of the Canadian development have a price tag of $64.5 million.

The additional electrical power made possible by the increased storage control is to be divided equally between the two countries. Canada has sold her share to public and private power companies (Columbia Storage and Power Exchange) for $254 million for first 30 years of the operation of each of the storage projects. Initially, a good bit of this electricity will find its way to the Southwest and California via the newly completed intertie. This system will utilize direct current transmission and represents a breakthrough in the technology of high voltage electrical transmission in the United States. This intertie represents a very important step in the development of the power potential of the Northwestern States as well as providing a stabilizing effect on the sequence and timing of new electrical generating facilities. The intertie will ultimately consist of more than the present single transmission line. To date, the largest share of the planning and construction costs are being borne by the Bonneville Power Administration and two private power companies.

Nuclear Power. Power from thermal nuclear generating plants is arriving on the scene much more rapidly than anticipated just a few years ago. Bonneville Power Administration estimates the Northwest will need 13 million kilowatts of nuclear or other thermal power by 1985. The 800,000 kilowatt generating plant at Hartford, Washington, built by the Washington Public Power System has been in operation since 1966. Its power output was oversubscribed by 71 public and cooperative electrical systems.

The Washington Public Power Supply System has already contracted with Westinghouse for a 1 million kilowatt turbine-generator nuclear unit for delivery in 1972 to be in service early in 1973. In a study prepared for the Bonneville Power Administration in 1967, sixteen possible sites were identified in the Pacific Northwest as possessing the characteristics necessary for nuclear plant developments. (See Figure 8). If these nuclear power plants are built with a capacity of a million kilowatts, the economies of scale achieved will be such that their electricity will be competitive with current hydro costs. While the demand for power in the Northwestern States is calculated to double in the next 10 years, the absorption of a million new kilowatts in any single consumer area would be an unlikely occurrence, but of course new generating plants must be ready to boost production exactly at the moment they are needed. This timing problem points to the wisdom of a large integrated regional power system and an interconnection with the voracious market of California and the Southwest. It is not inconceivable that sometime in the future a network of transmission lines will extend from southern California to Alaska.

Despite the appearance of a panacea for Northwestern power ills, nuclear power plants are viewed suspiciously by many of the inhabitants. In May, 1970 the voters of Eugene, Oregon turned down a nuclear power plant proposal which was to be located near Florence on the Oregon coast. Likewise, Seattle abandoned its Tiket Island nuclear site due to unfavorable public response. The concern for ecological equilibrium brought about by the national environmental quality movement of the 1970's and the seemingly ominous, unknown characteristics of nuclear energy probably has had a great deal to do with the reluctance being shown for nuclear power plants.

The generation of electricity by thermal means is almost entirely confined to the prospects of nuclear power in this region. The Central Washington Power Agency consisting of the Kittitas and Grant County Public Utility Districts recently abandoned their lease on coal deposits in the middle Washington Cascades after studies revealed that their costs were almost twice what they would have to be in order to compete with nuclear energy. At the same time, however, two private power companies are going ahead with a steam plant near Centralia, Washington, on the basis of 16,000 acres of coal beds which can be strip mined. In southern Oregon near Lakeview, numerous hot water geysers exist which might profitably be used in a thermal electric plant in conjunction with small amounts of additional fuel. This location is near the site of the Northwest-Southwest intertie which further enhances this possibility.

A recent development in turbine technology may tend to increase the hydro potential of the region. Tube type generators which are installed in inclined or horizontal positions rather than vertical require smaller excavation costs, can be utilized in circumstances where a smaller fall of water exists, and would have fewer problems associated with inundation for reservoirs. It is possible that this type of installation could be used on some of the tributaries of the major streams and may very well open up a whole new concept of water development, integrating power generation within relatively small water control districts which might even include irrigation and flood control as part of their functions.

Electrical Priorities. There is better than an even chance for a problem of major proportions to emerge from the necessity of the Bonneville Power Administration to invoke the preference clause of the Bonneville Act. (See page 56.) Conceivably, during the next ten years, some private power corporations may find themselves with reduced power availability due to the B.P.A.'s inability to serve both the needs of its preference customers and all others. Of the surplus power going into the power pool, the Bonneville Power Administration supplies about 35 percent while two other Public Utility Districts account for almost 60 percent. At present, the individual private power company deficits in the generation of electricity, which are made up by purchase from the surpluses in the power pool, range from a low of 3 percent to a high of 75 percent. In 1965, three of the eight private power customers of the Bonneville Power Administration made up generation deficits of over 50 percent from the power pool.[9]

The Bonneville Power Administration estimates that by 1975 most of the sites suitable for large hydroelectric projects will be developed and that subsequent to that date one million kilowatts of electricity will be needed within the region each year. It seems fairly clear that if all of the resources of both the people and the region are not brought to bear on this electrical growth problem serious consequences may result—not the least of which may be a decrease in power available from the B.P.A. for private power companies and their consumers due to the preference clause. The preference clause and the possibility of insufficient electricity may bring about a confrontation. From the point of view of the *consumer* of private power, why should he suffer the inconvenience of a power reduction simply because he happens to live in an area which is under the franchise of a private power company? The preference clause, in other words, discriminates not only between public and private electrical suppliers but also their customers.

The preferred status of the public power distribution entities over all other Bonneville Power Administration customers draws its rationale mainly from the common source of public finance. Apparently, non-profit utilities and taxpayers should benefit first from the public expenditure of tax dollars. While this argument seems logical

[9] U.S. Department of Interior, Bonneville Power Administration, *1965 Report, U.S. Columbia River System* (Dec. 1965).

when the sale of electricity generated by federal installations to other suppliers or distributors is being considered, it promptly accords a dilemma as far as individual consumers are concerned. As a rose is a rose, so is a federal taxpayer, whether a customer of a private power company or not. Does the federal agent for distribution of public domain power have an obligation to continue to serve all of its present consumers of power whether that power proceeds through public or privately owned distribution systems? It would seem to be arguable from the consumers' point of view. Probably not one in a thousand private power customers are aware of the preference clause and what its effect would be in the event of a decreased energy supply.

THE FUTURE AND SOME PROBLEMS

In some estimates, by the year 2,000 eleven and one half million people will be living in the Pacific Northwest with six million of them in the Willamette-Puget Trough between Everett, Washington, and Eugene, Oregon. Needless to say, if a population growth of this magnitude does occur it will present great demands on the water resources for increased power, domestic consumption, and assumably industrial and irrigation requirements as well. The interconnection of electrical transmission lines along the west coast would provide both the increased flexibility and power which would accompany such a growth. While this growth may or may not be achieved in the Northwest, it is evident that such characteristics already exist in California. One of the greatest controversies involving the water resource development of this region is shaping up in the form of various plans to transport surplus water from the Northwest to the Southwest and California. The North American Water and Power Alliance (NAWAPA) conceived by the engineering firm of Ralph M. Parsons is by far the most grandiose and detailed scheme.[10] Its design is aimed at a redistribution of the excess waters of the north-

[10] "North American Water and Power Alliance," Ralph M. Parsons Co. Brochure, #606–2934–19 (Los Angeles, California, 1965).

western part of the continent of North America and, as such, ranges throughout Canada, Alaska, the Western United States, and even includes developments in Mexico. Less ambitious plans such as those proposed by some California advocates simply call for a diversion of Snake River water to the south through a system of siphons and aqueducts utilizing the natural fall here and there for generating some electricity and thereby reducing the total costs of transporting the water. There is genuine fear on the part of those who are opposed to these large scale water transfers that insufficient water for further development within the region will result. An invocation of the "what if" plea is easy to make—"What if *we* should need it?" The same arguments were posed when proposals for sale of electricity to the Southwest were made.

The feeling of Northwestern ownership of these waters and their electrical products is exceedingly strong, and the notion of selling a naturally occurring commodity that exists in surplus like the iron ore of Minnesota simply does not exist. In part, this is no doubt a reaction to the Californians' nerve and audacity to covet "our water." There is no question that a study of water needs for the region should be made before serious thoughts are entertained for its disposal in the south, but so far the reaction has been the product of nervous energy and discussion of the problems generally creates more heat than light. The tendency for us to measure goodness in resource development as defined by past experiences is an affection for the status quo that may not be able to be tolerated much longer. It is a sort of curious anachronism that the visionary westerners have a severe case of myopia in this matter of sharing their water wealth. While a water resource is not exactly the same as an ore body, hoarding does not seem to fit the image of the reasonableness we seek either.

A recent piece of national legislation, championed by Senator Jackson of Washington, has as its principal purpose the establishing of a ten-year moratorium on the planning of diversion of waters from the Northwest. The intent of the Congress relative to this legislation is to "provide the recognition that each area of the country should have the opportunity to properly develop and plan the resources of their region." In effect, the message of this moratorium is that thou shalt not seek to appropriate your neighbor's water. The Northwestern water planners are thus free to develop their ideas for regional waters unfettered by the threat of outsiders for a period of ten years. It seems to have escaped the regional logicians that the main developable bodies of water within the area are subject to federal regulation inasmuch as they are navigable streams and could thus be considered as national rather than regional resources. Surely the interstate water agreements existing between state governments sharing a common drainage basin are the political forerunners of inter-regional agreements of a similar nature. One wonders what our reaction would have been to a ten-year planning moratorium invoked by British Columbia when we were considering the Upper Columbia River hydroelectric development.

While all agencies and states of the West need time to plan and assess their positions relative to their supply and demand for water, a piece of legislation that promotes the growth of these plans in isolation does not seem to be in the best interests of the allocation of our resources.

Unfortunately, water resource development has not been free of the political process. Water development projects are a fine source of public goodwill insofar as legislators are concerned, and differences in national administrations tend also to have direct effects on the course of events. When a Republican administration holds sway, the private sector is emphasized. License applications to build dams issued by the Federal Power Commission are then more favorable to the private power companies. The "partnership plan," whereby both federal and private developers combined to build a project, was the brainchild of the Eisenhower administration. While the partnership policy was not inherently a bad idea, in practice it became suspect. The business groups, for example, were able to contract for the revenue producing powerhouses and their equipment, while the cost of the remainder (and non-revenue producing) was borne by the government agencies. Also, during that administration there was a policy of "no new starts" insofar as the Corps of Engineers or Bureau of Reclamation were concerned. Under Democratic administrations the public and government applicants to the Federal Power Commission are more favorably treated, and public monies are expended to encourage and stimulate economic growth.

While differing views between major political parties is to be expected, an overriding policy pertaining to water resource development would seem a worthwhile venture. In the final analysis, it is the people who suffer the economic effects of political ambivalence in this field of development. Perhaps the newly formed Pacific Northwest River Basins Commission (replacing the Columbia Basin Inter-agency Committee) will find itself able to exert greater pressure in this regard under the Water Resources Planning Act of 1965.

RECLAMATION IRRIGATION

Reclamation irrigation projects demand the attention of the student of the Northwest from the point of view of their number, size, and complexity, and for their significance as factors in the economic growth of the region.

The hot and arid climatic environment that embraces the locale of most of the irrigation projects of the Northwest produces a landscape coloration of continuous grey. The sandy earth cover is grey, the sagebrush is grey, the weathered boards of abandoned homesteads are grey, even the jack-rabbits and sheep are grey. Windmills that were spaced so far apart that a person could scarcely see from one to the other, even in the flat country, coaxed water from hand-driven or dug wells for the sheep or goats that meandered about the countryside doing what was described as grazing. Periodically, windstorms swept this country scattering the herds, clogging water holes, and ruining the settler as surely as would the opening of his pocketbook to the wind. The purposeful transformation of this kind of a land certainly requires an imagination beyond that possessed by most of us.

Despite the absence of rain and organically rich soils, however, these lands are converted to productive agricultural plots by combining the warmth and long growing season with water, soils containing high proportions of soluble minerals, technology, and determination. In all, there are twenty-six irrigation projects sponsored by the Bureau of Reclamation within the region. They range in size from 3,000 acres to a potential 1,029,000 acres in the Columbia Basin Project. The Minidoka project in Idaho was the first to achieve authorization in 1904, followed by four others in 1905 (Boise, Idaho; Okanogan, Washington; Umatilla, Oregon; and Yakima, Washington).

In 1903, Theodore Roosevelt, speaking in behalf of the value of federal reclamation projects, said, "Most of the works contemplated for construction are of national importance, involving interstate questions, or the securing of self-supporting communities in the midst of vast tracts of vacant land. The nation as a whole is of course the gainer by the creation of these homes, adding as they do to the wealth and stability of the country, and furnishing a home market for the products of the East and South." [11] At this early stage in the development of enabling legislation, the frontier taming aspects associated with homesteading were strong motivating forces for the establishment of a settlement scheme for the arid west. A recurrence of strength in this attitude occurred after the ends of both World War I and II. A quiet return to the soil coupled with a move west must have been as much of a pilgrimage then as when the first settlers were arriving in Conestoga wagons. Going to a new western land had a certain mystical purpose which may not have been much different from Thoreau's in going to Walden Pond: "My purpose . . . was not to live cheaply nor to live dearly there, but to transact some private business with the fewest obstacles."

When subjected to the scrutiny of financial feasibility, however, the frontier-like charismatic quality of reclamation irrigation fades

[11] Congressional Record, 58th Congress, 2nd Session (December 7, 1903), p. 7.

away quite rapidly. These irrigation projects are not a simple means of providing new homes and more food for the nation. They represent, in fact, one of the most technical and costly forms of the agricultural enterprise. It has been discovered, for example, that reclamation irrigation water users contribute to only about one-third of the costs of projects directly attributable to the irrigation system.[12] The rest of the repayment is generally met by power revenues. Many of those reclamation projects in the Northwest, which either do not have a power generating facility or contribute in some way to power generation (storage or regulation) in conjunction with the irrigation project, have experienced difficulties (some of major proportions) in meeting their financial obligations of repayment. Some of the more outspoken critics of the reclamation projects call them drainage projects rather than irrigation projects, referring to the almost universal problems of drainage that arise. On the Columbia Basin Project in Washington, the increased costs attributable to drainage problems caused principally by the irrigators led to a lengthy debate between the irrigators and the Bureau of Reclamation. Initially, the farmers resisted any increases in their repayment contracts and insisted instead that the additional drainage costs be added to the construction charges to be paid for by power revenues from the sale of electricity from Grand Coulee Dam. This type of subsidy to irrigation agriculture is no different in spirit from others provided throughout the economic fabric of the nation, but some feel that "honesty in packaging" could be a little more strictly adhered to. The Bureau of Reclamation could be accused of a little naiveness when their projects almost consistently cost more than their estimates; sometimes considerably more. Social and economic progress costs money, but we should be as informed as possible about project feasibility and water efficiency to see that greater wastes than necessary are not being accommodated. In fairness, there are a good many factors over which the Bureau has no control, not the least of which

[12] U.S. Gov't. Printing Office, *Reclamation, Accomplishments and Contributions,* Report by the Library of Congress Legislative Reference Service, Washington, 1959.

is legislative appropriations. Projects that take ten years or more to complete will naturally have rising cost complications.

At this point, one other illustration will be useful in adding perspective to the financial aspects of Northwestern irrigation agriculture. Usually, the existence and extent of competition between suppliers of raw materials are fair indicators of the economic health of an industry governed by private enterprise. Accordingly, the extent to which operators vie for the privilege of supplying water for irrigation purposes should reflect to some extent the economic state of irrigation. In 1959, in the entire four states of Washington, Oregon, Idaho, and Montana, there were only three commercial irrigation plants. Another meaningful observation is the fact that all of the Western states having over 500,000 acres of irrigated agricultural lands have experienced a downward trend in the number of commercial water suppliers. For example, from 1940 to 1959, California went from 104 to 51, Colorado from 53 to 4.[13] No matter what the specific reasons may be—consolidation, Bureau of Reclamation competition, or whatever—the predominant recurring theme seems to be that of cost. High and increasing costs of irrigation agricultural production have caused a reevaluation of the opportunities for the investment of private resources, both capital and land.

Some economic forecasters in the state of Washington have entertained the notion that the state should begin to assume some of the responsibility for the development of its lands that have irrigation agriculture potential. While it may seem impertinent, perhaps it would be more wise to investigate the possibility of investing in this enterprise in California. For one thing, a state's pattern of financial behavior is more like a corporation's than the federal government's, expecting its investments to produce income in a fairly short period of time. For another, in the light of the repayment schedules for Bureau of Reclamation Irrigation Projects in the Northwest, the possibility of committing a gross political error is

[13] U.S. Dep't. of Commerce, Bureau of Census, U.S. Census of Agriculture, 1959, *Irrigation of Agricultural Lands,* vol. III, pp. 30–32.

quite likely. The reasonableness of the enterprise for investor-owned capital seems rather well defined by the almost nonexistent commercial activity previously mentioned.

Perhaps it may be possible to plan small, highly integrated plots in conjunction with other resource developments as the previously mentioned inclined tube type generators. There is not much question that irrigated plots are desirable in the Northwest, offering as they do a measure of control over the natural forces. Due to their intensive nature, however, the manipulation of productive factors causes them to be more like manufacturing plants than agricultural enterprises, and an allocation of resources for their development must be based on more than the known permissiveness of the natural environment. Physical possibility is not tantamount to economic feasibility.

Columbia Basin Irrigation Project. The Columbia Basin Project is the largest Bureau of Reclamation undertaking in the United States. At present, a little more than half of the 1,029,000 acres originally planned for inclusion in the project have been developed. The original estimate for its cost was approximately $754.5 million, but in 1963 when another estimate was made of the cost of the construction it totalled $961 million. Additional drainage appurtenances alone added $634,000 to the cost. It would not be surprising to this observer if the final cost were nearer to $1⅛ billion, assuming that the entire area originally planned for the project does, in fact, become a part of the development. If, however, there is such a thing as marginal land in the nomenclature of irrigable land, then surely since the inception of this project in the 1930s and implementation of settlement in the 1940s, some of those original one million acres have passed into economic marginality. It would seem unusual that the principle of diminishing returns did not operate in the field of irrigation agriculture.

The role of this project as a stimulus to economic development is undeniable. The net farm income in 1963 was about $30 million for the project area. When compared to an adjacent dryland agricultural area, the basin project produced almost four times more net farm income per acre of cropland.[14] After fifteen years of operation, every indicator of economic growth points to a successful impact on the region by the project. Federal income taxes paid, assessed property values, population growth, increasing wage totals, and other similar guides all point to significant economic gains.

The part that Grand Coulee Dam plays in the expanded economy of the region must be considered as a positive influence as well, since it is an integral part of the reclamation project. Since 1941, the estimated gross revenue produced by Grand Coulee power sales alone was nearly $500 million. When the indirect benefits of cost-benefit ratio analyses are considered, even in the most gross and imperfect manner, the financial influence of the dam and project takes on even greater significance. The dependency on the multiplying effect of government financed projects to achieve the threshold of regional economic puberty has resulted in the success that was hoped for by the early planners.

The undetermined and perhaps indeterminable question is, however, whether this investment provides the most reasonable allocation of the capital, land, and water resources required. A Northwesterner's bias toward an affirmative answer is really quite obvious when the extent of public works in the region is reviewed, but the notion that there are alternative uses for those resources is a realization that must be coped with. How economic history will treat this resource allocation and its developments is a matter yet to be decided.

The manner in which a region's scarce resources are used in the initial phases of economic development oftentimes is such that maximum benefits, as defined by the most profitable method of implementation, are foregone in order to increase employment opportunities. In a region like the Northwest, it has been a mundane, academic exercise to point out that study after study shows that in terms of value added, the industrial demands for water in manufacturing

---

[14] Washington Agricultural Experiment Station, Washington State University. *The Economic Significance of Columbia Basin Project Development.* Bulletin 669 (Sept. 1966).

leads all other potential users. Heretofore, what would be manufactured, for whom, and at what price? As the region has matured, however, so has regional industrialization, and whereas earlier there was little or no competition for water, the economic diversification brought on by this maturity has now ushered in a new phase in the progression of economic development. Water used for irrigation is now being looked at more critically as alternatives for its use become real competitors. Regional markets are expanding and manufacturing has gained a toehold in the economic scheme of things.

SUMMARY

The major thrust of this chapter has been to focus attention on the dominant features of the role of water resources in this region's development. This has not been an exhaustive sojourn and such problems as water quality have been ignored in favor of presenting the case for water resource development as the cornerstone of regional growth and calling attention to the oncoming necessity for a change in the evaluative processes whose end is to render decisions about water utilization.

5   *The Gainful Use of the Land*

THE CHARACTERISTICS of the Pacific Northwest's land base and the region's economic immaturity sometimes combine to produce a nearly static environmental condition that allows alteration in resource dependencies and internal economic adjustments to occur at a rate that could almost be described as viscous.

Forests cover almost half of the region and are associated with the settlement inhibiting factor of mountains. Eighty-five percent of the area is unsuited to cultivation, and of the 15 percent that is, three-quarters is in the worst two categories of land capability classes of the Soil Conservation Service. Only about 32 percent of the farmland is actually harvested cropland which is an indication of the intensity of use that is possible. Climate plays a part in limiting the alternatives for land use, also, for approximately one-third of the region is categorized as either steppe or desert.

Large blocks of land remain within the province of public owner ship and thus are not as susceptible to the economic flux which brings about change in land use. The Forest Service, National Park Service, Bureau of Land Management, and the individual states are responsible for the administration of over half of the total area. Public domain programs based on such principles as sustained yield forestry and reforestation are obviously committed to the long run. Thus these resources do not respond to market changes as rapidly as those governed by commercial ownership.

As mentioned previously, the geographic division of labor of the Pacific Northwest has resulted in a pattern of regional specialization that has a strong orientation toward the extractive industries. When seen from the point of view of economic land uses this specialization resolves itself into six main groupings with four sub-groups. Forestry and its allied industries, recreation-tourism, mining and metallurgical processing, agriculture and food processing, fisheries, and transportation equipment are the main categories, with agriculture having the four subcategories of special significance. These are dryland wheat, irrigated specialties, dairying, and livestock raising.

FORESTRY

The states of Washington and Oregon contain the largest portions of commercial forestlands in the region. These areas contain about 35 percent of the nation's supply of sawtimber. The most valuable tree species are Douglas Fir and Western Hemlock west of the Cascades, while Ponderosa Pine, White Pine, Western Larch, and Douglas Fir are the most important east of the Cascades. (Western Larch and Douglas Fir surpassed Ponderosa Pine in their use in lumber production in Western Montana about 1950.)

In terms of national production of board feet of lumber, Oregon leads the Western States providing 25 percent of the total while California is second with 15 percent, Washington third with 11 percent and Idaho last with 5 percent. During the past 25 years, Washington has registered an overall decline in lumber production while Idaho has been increasing its share. Ownership of the marketable timber is divided about evenly between private lumber companies and the National Forests.

Taken as a whole, the forest industries vie with agriculture as the number one income producer of the Northwest, followed by recreation-tourism. Lumber and wood products comprise about 25 percent of the total value added by manufacture in the region, and the forest products industries employ over half of the people engaged in manufacturing. About half of the railroad freight traffic that originates in the region is involved with forest products of one kind or another. The largest share of Northwest production is marketed in the Midwestern and Northeastern Atlantic States with California and local markets being next largest. The greatest single cause of fluctuation in production is variability in the building trades, particularly dwellings.

Dramatic changes have occurred in the forest products industries in the last twenty years. While the technological innovations of the chain saw and bulldozer have been making the conversion of trees to logs almost child's play, engineering inventiveness at the mill sites has been providing more efficient use of raw materials, resulting in a wider variety of wood products. Larger sawmills were built to take better advantage of the large size of old growth timber, giving advantages in economies of scale not able to be realized elsewhere in the United States. For instance, in 1962, 72 percent of the production of the West was accounted for by 373 mills, each producing 15 million board feet.[15] Large integrated plants producing lumber, paper, plywood, presto logs, and composition board are becoming more common as the industry tools up for the task of increasing production to meet the demands of the next twenty years.

In that regard, the Northwest is in an enviable position. According to some projections, a decline of about 20 percent will occur in the region's inventory of sawtimber by the year 2000. This sawtimber is mostly old growth, however, and does not make the most efficient use of the space wherein it grows. Once it is cut and reforestation takes place, man will improve on nature's productiveness and even greater yields will be realized from the same forest plot. If production demands of the future are to be met, it is almost necessary that the old growth areas be cut and reforested according to a systematic, well-timed plan. While this region possesses about one-third of the country's growing stock of timber and over 50 percent of the nation's softwood sawtimber, its resources will be strained if projections of demand for future wood products are correct.

Reforestation. The annual investment in reforestation programs in Oregon and Washington has increased considerably since 1949.

---

[15] Federal Reserve Bank of San Francisco, "Lumber: Out on a Limb?" *Monthly Review* (December 1964), p. 249.

The largest amounts are being spent by public agencies as they try to reduce the extent of unstocked commercial forestland under their respective jurisdictions. The figures to be dealt with are deceptive, but it is probably safe to say that approximately two million acres of unstocked lands exist in Washington and Oregon, and, according to some estimates, this is the remainder of a three million acre unstocked inventory of lands which existed thirty years ago. Direct seeding of trees is favored over the planting of seedlings now as the costs are considerably less in most cases.

The part that reforestation plays in the future inventory of marketable timber will be no less important than other schemes devised to increase the total production of the region.

Conservation and Multiple Use. The forest industry has been one of the most stalwart in its support of the ideas of conservation. The public information programs of the foresters have probably been more effective than any other in bringing to the attention of the inhabitants of the Northwest the nature of the symbiotic relationships between natural resources and people.

The forest industry also has been largely responsible for changing public attitudes from "woodsman spare that tree" to "wise use" insofar as the meaning of conservation is concerned. From that point, it took only minor adjustments to fit the notion of multiple use of water resource development into the context of forestry. Accordingly, forestlands have not only been looked upon as a source of wood products, but are manipulated to benefit watershed management, wildlife, grazing, recreation, and the prevention of erosion.

As with the case of water resources, however, the increasing intensity of some uses has caused planners to reevaluate the relative demands of all of them. Grazing in the National Forests has been greatly reduced, and special hunts have been authorized where game animals have caused young tree losses that were deemed excessive. The old notion of a widespread protectionism associated with the kind and gallant forest ranger has given way to a kind but firm forest manager whose knowledge not only includes forest lore, but plant taxonomy and ecology as well.

Some Problems. The Pacific Northwest forest industry faces several very perplexing problems. Canadian lumber imports into the Eastern States are causing increased competition and consternation within the western lumber industry. Exports from British Columbia have increased considerably in the last few years. For all practical purposes, all of the natural advantages previously mentioned that accrue to the Pacific Northwest forest industry are also true for British Columbia since its forest is simply a northern extension of the Northwest's. One of the major problems associated with this increased Canadian competition centers around the Jones Act of 1920, which stipulates that all intercoastal shipments of lumber produced in the United States must move in U.S. ships in that commerce. Canada has no such restraints. Both the loading charges and charter rates are higher for domestic shipping than others and, as a result, this tithe to the merchant marine compounds the problems of the local lumber producer. Couple this with the fact that there is internal competition in the forest industries caused by new building materials, such as plywood, and it becomes easy to see how the small sawmill operator producing only dimension lumber is being squeezed none too gently into economic oblivion. (The lumber industry has not gained proportionately from the growth in housing demand in the last few years because of competition with plywood, gypsum wallboard, and other similar building materials. This seems ominous for the smaller lumber manufacturers.)

Another problem involving shipping is that of exporting logs to Japan. This exportation has been an extremely controversial issue. It centers around the ability of the Japanese to offer higher prices for low quality logs than domestic producers, transport them home in their own ships, and return with finished goods to compete successfully in the U.S. market. Over half of the principal export tree types were Western Hemlock and almost all were of the poorer quality of sawmill logs. In a study done by the Forest Service, it was found that in four out of six Washington and Oregon ports where exporting was taking place the value of the logs was greater for export than for their value if used in domestic manufacturing.[16] Home industry has prevailed, however, and the export restrictions on logs from the National Forests to Japan has become effective. The fact that Canada and Siberia could both readily supply the Japanese demand did not seem to deter this decision; neither did the observation that large private timber holdings would tend to reduce the effect of a public tree embargo. This seems yet another example of the Northwesterners' provincialism.

Air and water pollution are problems associated principally with the pulp and paper mills of the region. For years there has been little recourse for residents living adjacent to plants that produced offensive smells, smoke, and vapors having possible harmful effects. In addition, the effluent from these mills was the largest source of pollutants in the streams and coastal waters of the region. Public nuisance laws offered little in the way of possible pollution abatement, and companies either ignored the clamor of public opinion or assuaged it with token control measures. The costs involved in pulp mill pollution control were indeed great, but they were a poor excuse for inaction and threats of moving to other states where people were not so fussy. The Water Quality Act of 1965 cleared the way for states to establish pollution control standards and for the federal government to participate in control measures involving interstate waters. Finally, problems that had been defined and responsibility assigned for five years or more began to be solved. In the meantime, shellfish beds were adversely affected by pulp and paper mill wastes along the northern Washington coast, salmon fisherman lost time, gear, and fish in the collection of slime and fibers on their nets in the lower Columbia, and smog and smell were endured by people living near these plants.

[16] Adams and Hamilton, *Value and Employment Associated with Pacific Northwest Log Exports.* Pacific Northwest Forest and Range Experiment Station, U.S.D.A., U.S. Forset Service Research Paper PNW 27, 1965.

Just as there is increased competition between the multiple uses of water, so are there problems of this nature in the forest preserves. The question of wilderness recreation versus timber production is one of the most difficult, for it seems to be strongly related to the intricacies of the "Northwestern Mystique"—that live-in but let-alone attitude toward the physical environment. Even in the face of such overwhelming statistics of value ratios as high as 17 to 1 in favor of timber production over wilderness recreation, groups of people flock to public hearings and stubbornly insist that these benefits should be foregone in favor of the pristine wilderness. On the other hand, some businessmen simply cannot understand the point of view that irrespective of timber values the esthetic value is at least equal if not greater. Since these values cannot be measured very closely in dollars and cents, an argumentative reliance must be made on the reasonableness for a sanctuary wherein it is possible for recreation to recreate.

The value per se of recreation areas in the wilderness is rarely questioned, but the size of prospective parks sometimes is, along with the foresters' legitimate concern that totally wild areas could be sources of fire, disease, and pest dangers as they are left to develop in their natural state. Technically, they could thus present a real threat to surrounding commercial forestlands, to say nothing of the self destruction of the recreation area. It would seem as though this is yet another case that calls for diligence in the art of compromise.

To sum up, the Northwest's oldest industry has changed considerably from the days of spars, poles, and board lumber. The principles of allowable cut and sustained yield stand in stark contrast to the "cut and get out" attitude that was responsible for the exploitation of the forests of Michigan. The industry has become highly diversified and conscious of efficiency in production. This has resulted in increasing numbers of large mills that have combined many of the productive operations of the forest industries at one site.

A customarily resource-oriented industry (in terms of the location of their plants) has even broken that tradition in the location of a pulp and paper mill at Attalia, Washington, which is surrounded not by trees but by sagebrush and desert. It sits athwart rail lines that go in four directions and the slack water transportation system of the Columbia River and thus has the accessibility it needs for both raw materials and markets.

As is the case with agriculture, the forest industry today is typified by increasing efforts toward intensification and pre-harvest inputs. The changes undergone in the industry have had an important stabilizing effect on the economic growth of the region.

RECREATION-TOURISM

The Pacific Northwest has the greatest recreational potential of any region in the nation. The landscape is so diversified and space so uncongested that it offers innumerable possibilities for recreational activities while still maintaining the basis for the mental seclusion that people seek in "getting away from it all."

The fact that the Northwesterners are ardent admirers of their own landscape is confirmed by the fact that they spend more of their leisure time in their own region than do residents of other regions and that expenditures of state and local governments for recreational purposes amounts to about $55 million annually.[17]

As a revenue producing industry, recreation has some very intriguing aspects. At present, it is the fourth ranking employer of the region. Tourists spend about $900 million annually within the region with five-eighths coming from regional residents and three-eighths from out-of-state visitors. If the present trend of expansion continues, by 1985 recreation-tourism may be the second or third ranking industry of the region. It is not inconceivable that it could attain the rank of number one.

The mountain and forestlands, which curtail the extent of arable land, do provide the basis for economic growth along other lines. At the present time, the recreational hinterland of this region extends about 500 miles from its borders, or approximately one day's travel

[17] U.S. Department of Interior, Bonneville Power Administration, *Pacific Northwest Economic Base Study—Recreation,* vol. 2, part 9.

time by automobile. The visitor statistics compiled by state and federal agencies all indicate rapidly increasing rates of facilities' use. Practically all tourists travel to the region by car, and this mode of behavior no doubt will be intensified as five highways of the new national interstate system enter the region from adjacent states. Altogether there are approximately twelve million people in this recreational hinterland, but more importantly these adjacent areas are enjoying very rapid population growth. A 34 percent increase took place in these areas during the period 1950–1960, while the Pacific Northwest gained only 17½ percent and the nation as a whole 18½ percent.

Since the recreation industry is one which relies heavily on public sources for development capital, it tends to be sluggish in its response to increasing demand. There is no industry in existence that would not revel at the thought of having the growth curves that are associated with *every* aspect of Northwestern recreation and tourism. The increasing pressure on existing facilities is causing some deterioration and will no doubt hasten further development, but continued investment needs to be expedited at every opportunity. As a recreation region, the Northwest enjoys a favorable balance of trade, so to speak, and one way to intensify this already beneficial situation would be to invest even more heavily in the regional recreational enterprise. Increasing fiscal demands for schools and other services are straining the ability of property taxes to maintain even current levels of expenditures. The development of the recreational resources would seem well suited to ease the taxpayers' burden.

The recreation and tourist industries are admirably suited to the Northwesterners' state of mind. They are industries that do not contribute to the overpopulating of the region, they do not create air and water pollution problems, there is little diminution of the resource if proper management is exercised, and they require only developmental and maintenance capital. The Northwestern recreational resources have all of the profit aspects of a gambling casino without the expense of either the building or the games. As per capita income and leisure time both increase, an undeveloped recreational potential will mean foregoing even greater benefits than perhaps the region can afford.

It seems incongruous to think of the snowy crests of the Olympics and Cascades as the counterpart of a Las Vegas or Monaco in terms of a source of revenue, and heavy commercialization of recreational resources would probably incite the inhabitants' ire beyond reconciliation. Some means will have to be found to discover how much development is possible before it begins to detract from the users' recreational purposes.

The most problematical conflicts associated with the development of recreational resources are those that are involved with the mutually exclusive uses of wilderness reservations and the lumber or mining interests. In the preceding section, reference has already been made to the problems of commercial forest maintenance and the businessman's point of view regarding wilderness preserves.

For the most part, economic exploitation and recreation exist side by side with a minimum of conflict in this region. Occasionally, however, a circumstance arises that pits one against the other, and when it does it usually emerges as a battle in which preservation is at stake. A mining company owning a claim or patent naturally observes that under the law it has the right of exploitation subject only to the principles of supply and demand and regulations concerning the use of the public domain—and, furthermore, the country needs the minerals. A recreationist is quick to point out that tariffs protecting the mineral industries make a mockery of supply and demand, and the laying waste to a particularly unique or beautiful natural site amounts to an additional subsidy that is entirely out of proportion insofar as the existence of the mining company is concerned. A "Remove Mount Rainier Park so the Black Iron Company can Compete" campaign probably would not find many supporters in the Pacific Northwest, although this is not always the case. Sometimes the residents of potential mining or logging areas become quite irritated with people who support wilderness preservation proposals for their regions because these plans would mean their foregoing of jobs and income.

Once established, there is a tendency, too, for us to view a recreational haven as having to exist forever in that state. It should be observed that recreation sites also make serviceable reservations for more intensive land uses that might be identified and deemed to be of greater importance than recreation in the future.

MINING AND METALLURGICAL PROCESSING

The search for gold and silver in forms that could be easily recovered brought settlement to the Northwest before it would have occurred otherwise. In a great number of places, the settling effect was only transitory, and ghost towns are all that remain of the original sites of places, some of which once knew the clamor of as many as 5,000 people. The fortunes and misfortunes of Northwestern mining make up a history that is as colorful and exciting as can be found anywhere.

The Coeur d'Alene district, the Salmon and Snake rivers in Idaho, the Powder and John Day rivers in Oregon, and the Blewett Pass and Republic areas of Washington were all sites where gold fever was running high in the middle and late 1800s. Initially, placer and lode gold received the most attention, along with lode silver. As time passed, minerals such as lead and zinc, which were found in association with many silver ores, attracted the attention of the mining investors, and some mining camps gradually gave way to one street boardwalk towns, marking the end of the initial phase of mineral discovery and exploitation.

The list of mineral occurrences in the region is quite impressive, but, of course, not all are of economic significance. Of the metallic minerals, lead, zinc, silver, copper, and gold are the most important. Mineral fuels (other than uranium ores) are the region's most scarce and least valuable, while building and construction minerals are most abundant and of the greatest value. The metallic minerals fall somewhere in between with the production ranking as follows: copper, lead, silver, gold, and zinc. In terms of national production, Idaho is the first ranking producer of silver and antimony, Montana achieves that status with manganese, and Oregon with nickel. From the standpoint of value of production, the ignoble construction materials of sand, gravel, stone, and cement are the principal minerals of Washington, Oregon, and western Montana (with the notable exception of copper), while silver, lead, and zinc are the most valuable in Idaho.[18] For comparative purposes, the entire value of mineral production of Washington, Oregon, and Idaho is approximately equal to one-third the farm value of production for the state of Washington, or roughly equivalent to its wheat and milk production.

Mineral Fuels. The absence of mineral fuels in large exploitable quantities is one of the more outstanding characteristics of the region. While coal exists in both Washington and Oregon, it has not been an important source of fuel since near the end of World War II, when competition for stoker coal from Utah and conversion to diesel electric rail engines caused a major slump in consumption. Some domestic coals could be used for the production of coke. However, it would be quite costly and the present economic matrix of regional steel production probably precludes the support of a blast furnace at this time.

Petroleum has been discovered within the region, but so far not to the extent that it would encourage investment by the prudent man. The noted Sunshine Mining Company of Idaho silver fame has two wells in Grays Harbor, Washington, which were completed in 1957. A total of 12,500 barrels of oil were pumped between 1957 and 1961 when they were shut down. Three other wells were put down in the same area between 1947 and 1951 with each producing only a hundred barrels or so before being closed. This kind of production is a far cry from a California production figure of 300 million barrels annually or even Montana's 30 million. The Grays Harbor oil was to be refined in Tacoma and a royalty of 12½ percent on the gross sales of oil produced was to be received by the state of Washington.

Natural gas in commercial quantities must be imported into the

18 U.S. Department of Commerce, *Statistical Abstract of the United States,* 1966.

region from the Southwest and Canada, as unprofitable regional fields lie undeveloped.

Lead, Zinc, Copper, Aluminum. Lead, zinc, copper, and aluminum provide the core for a mineral industries development within the region of modest proportions. The Berkeley open pit mine at Butte, Montana, has been one of the oldest and most productive sources for copper ore in the region. Most of the known reserves for copper exist in this area. Butte ore is refined at Great Falls and smeltered at Anaconda, Montana. Some wire and rod are produced near the mill site, with the rest divided between exports and Eastern U.S. consumers. Another large copper smelter and refinery is located at Tacoma, Washington, where ores from the Philippines, Canada, South America, and Newfoundland are treated. This complex is known as a custom operation since it is not directly connected with a mine of its own and must rely on competing in the open market for ore to process. Most of its products have foreign markets located in both Europe and the Far East.

The Holden mine near Lake Chelan in Washington was the only other producer of copper within the region, and it was closed down in 1957. A potential production area belonging to the Kennecott Copper Company exists in the high Cascades of Washington in the Glacier Peak Wilderness Area. A controversy of major proportions is still raging over the possible development of this site—one of the most spectacular landscapes in the Northwest.

Competition from aluminum has made some inroads into the copper market of the Northwest for such things as aerial high voltage transmission lines. Aluminum is both lighter in weight and lower in cost. It is not equal or better in its conductivity characteristics, however, and the recent trend toward the burial of municipal power lines is favorable to the copper market.

Butte, the Coeur d'Alene district of Idaho, and Metaline, Washington, are the main areas of production for lead and zinc. By far the most important is the Idaho region as its production merits a national industrial rating. The number of lead and zinc mines has been decreasing as Northwestern production tends to have higher costs associated with its extraction and processing than other domestic producers. Part of this problem is related to the age of the mines, for discoveries began here in the 1880s. Distance to domestic markets has already been established as an inhibiting factor.

Both the Metaline and Coeur d'Alene district mines are of the underground variety and experience the difficulties and added costs associated with depth and ventilation. While there are numerous lead-zinc mines spread across northeastern Washington and northern Idaho, the greatest portion of production comes from just seven mines. Recent interest in lead connected with improved markets has stimulated the local mining interests of these areas considerably. Speculation is increasing with the interest being shown in the development of an electric car that would utilize larger quantities of lead in the batteries.

The Northwestern lead and zinc smeltering industry may be finding itself in a bit of a dilemma. Domestic and foreign ore imports have been of great importance in their scheme of production because the local mining production did not match smelter capacities necessary for an economic operation. The growing tendency for foreign ore suppliers to increase the value of their products by smeltering at home prior to export places the Northwestern smelter in the position of having to purchase more domestic ore, which is of higher cost. If regional consumption and domestic mining production can be increased, this change will not have such a harsh effect on the industry.

Aluminum. The aluminum industry came to the Northwest during the early phases of World War II, in response to the war needs in aircraft manufacture and the availability of cheap, federally-generated, electrical power for the conversion of alumina to the metal. In 1940 there was only one mill in the region, located at Vancouver, Washington, but shortly thereafter five government owned plants and a rolling mill were erected in Washington and Oregon. These plants were subsequently disposed of by the government after the war, with private companies and the region being the benefactors. Aluminum production has continued ever since, but not without some serious interruptions during the 1950s. A general decline in production in Northwestern mills occurred then as the development of cheap electricity in Texas, through the use of natural gas, and a shortage of interruptible power in the Northwestern region combined to reduce the advantage of inexpensive regional hydroelectricity. The eternal problem of depressed local consumption and long distances from principal markets were also factors in this decline. Optimistic overbuilding of plant capacity probably should be added to the list as well.

Since that time, both local and national markets have increased considerably, as has the supply of large blocks of regional low cost electricity. Shipping costs have decreased to some extent, but the most important factor is the renewed availability of electricity, as the region again is able to provide this industrial electricity at a low cost.

The raw material for the aluminum reduction works is moved into the region by both water and rail transportation. Malayan ore finds its way to The Dalles, Oregon, by way of Japan and Portland, Oregon. A new International Aluminum Company plant at Bellingham, Washington, will use alumina from Australia, as will the Kaiser plants in Spokane and Tacoma.

The aluminum industry of this region will continue to prosper so long as the necessary quantities of electricity are made available to it at prices it can afford. The relationship between this necessity and increased regional electrical development is obvious.

Steel. The production of steel in the Pacific Northwest accounts for less than one half of one percent of the national steel ingot capacity. Good grades of iron ore are conspicuously absent and coking coals are limited to those encountering high costs of manufacture.

Steel making has been confined to scrap materials for the basic charge, the most favored being items of comparatively high density and low in impurities, such as decommissioned ships. The earliest mills used oil fired blast furnaces, but these have given way to electrolytic furnaces. At present, the reduction works are located in the Seattle and Portland areas. Steel bars and plate are the principal products, the largest share being used in the construction trades.

The Pacific Northwest steel market is estimated to be 70 percent greater than regional production, so it would appear that a regional increase is in order. Any new development would have to include rolling mills producing a wider variety of products than at present and reduction plants that utilized the least expensive rather than the most expensive means of converting the raw materials to metals. It is possible that change brought about by technology may make ore reduction plants economically feasible at some time in the future. Meanwhile, the possibility that good quality scrap metals may become more scarce should not be overlooked. Ability to compete for this raw material in the open markets could prove to be the most influential factor in continuing even the present levels of production.

The entire minerals industry of the region employs approximately 39,000 people or about 2 percent of the labor force, most of whom are in the aluminum and copper industries. The mining segment, where unbridled optimism is still the most potent motivating force, is the least changed aspect of the industry. This attitude is typified by the Big Basin Oil Company's motto: "One good speculation is worth a lifetime of work." Almost without exception the nondiversification so common to the mining communities is responsible for their retarded economic development. One wonders if towns were left to choose, how many would select mining as their mode of economic support?

The manufacturing and processing portions of the minerals industry are those that have changed the most since the early days, for they tend to be market oriented and have combined their fate with that of the urban landscape where social and economic changes are occurring the most rapidly.

AGRICULTURE AND FOOD PROCESSING

The agricultural industry of the Northwestern States is second only to the forest industries in its economic significance. Viewing the industry broadly, one is struck by the diversity it exhibits. Even though only 15 percent of the land is suitable for cultivation, a wide variety of crops are grown. In large measure, this is due to variability in the climate, fortuitous land and soil circumstances, and the artificial environment provided by irrigation projects. Within this pattern of diversity, there exists considerable specialization made possible by regional economic reciprocity and the well developed national system of transportation. Farm activities range from the intensive agricultural types of irrigated hops to the extensive type characterized by the dryland wheat monoculture areas.

There is a definite tendency toward reliance on cash crops having relatively high per unit values, particularly in the irrigation projects, and regional farms characteristically have large investments in both machinery and land.

The largest share of agricultural production is committed to areas whose natural soil conditions must be improved to some extent if yields commensurate with inputs are to be obtained. The only notable exceptions are the Willamette-Puget Trough and the Palouse areas where the soils are inherently quite fertile. Soil maintenance practices are obligatory on all croplands.

Dryland Wheat. Dryland wheat, one of the four agricultural regional specializations previously identified, is produced on immense farms, many of which exceed 2,000 acres in size. The Palouse region of east-central Washington is the most highly touted area of production, for the rolling loess hills boost the regional average yield to forty bushels to the acre. Research in wheat hybridization has continued to help the wheat farmers produce greater yields on the same number of acres that for a time produced agricultural surplus headaches. With the newest of wheat innovations, the Gaines variety, average regional yields will probably top fifty bushels to the acre— about twice the national average. In general, the recent crop yields are expected to be about 30 percent greater than those of five years ago due to both increased acreages and the various efforts of intensification.

The Palouse wheat farmer is inclined to have received more education than his counterpart in the other phases of Northwestern agriculture and it shows in his willingness to experiment and in his keeping abreast of the changes brought about by agricultural research that will improve his livelihood. Nevertheless, soil erosion problems continue to be serious in the Palouse as well as the other dryland wheat areas. While deep gullying is not a common sight, sheet, rill, and minor gully erosion are. Wind erosion in the central Washington and Oregon wheat fields removes as much as three inches of topsoil a year, causing dust storms at frequent intervals.

The climatic circumstance favors winter wheat growing with the soft varieties being raised almost exclusively. Although the region produces a surplus, it is a net importer of wheat as the hard varieties from eastern Montana and elsewhere are necessary to produce a blend for bread flours.

Mechanization on the wheat farm is personified by the self-propelled combine, a $16,000 harvesting machine that is used less than thirty days a year.

Only a short time ago, harvested Northwestern wheat could be found in many odd places—in old ships, abandoned buildings, any place that offered the rudiments of shelter. Surplus wheat and wealthy wheat farmers, who could not go wrong because of government subsidies, were the recipients of much verbal abuse and the cause of many protracted arguments. Now, largely through foreign aid programs, the surpluses have disappeared and the national agricultural industries look as though they may be hard pressed to keep many of the world's people from starvation diets.

In response to a 1969 downturn in wheat prices and a contemporaneous upturn in the value of beef, some of the marginal dryland wheat areas are commencing a change in land use. In southeastern Washington, some wheatland is being converted to hay and forage crops to exploit this market change.

Irrigated Agricultural Specialties. The fame of Washington apples, Idaho potatoes, and Oregon pears is such that no further exposition is necessary. The irrigation environment in which they prosper is provided mainly by the Bureau of Reclamation. Hops used for beer flavoring are a specialty of the Yakima Valley area and provide the state of Washington with a status of number one ranking in production. In good years, the hop production represents the highest per unit value crop of the region, averaging between $600 and $700 per acre in contrast to about $80 for wheat. The famed Washington apples come from a series of highland rim valleys along the east slopes of the Cascade Mountains and the north-south trending valleys of the Okanogan Highlands.

Since Cuba no longer represents a source for sugar, the beet sugar production on Northwestern irrigated lands has expanded. There had been constant agitation under the former provisions of the Sugar Act to extend the sugar production allotments to newly developed irrigated lands, since it was a crop that was assured a market and could thereby provide an economic boost to the new farmers. Sinecures are few in farming, but the reduction of risk provided by irrigation and the increased size of a guaranteed sugar market, resulting from Cuba's absence from the American sugar scene, just about amounted to that. Farm mortgages of $50,000 to $80,000 are not uncommon on newly settled irrigation lands here, however, and it would seem reasonable to apply such measures of economic relief as are feasible. The irrigation farmers of Idaho produce the largest value of production for both sugar beets and potatoes, while Washington's are the major producers of hops and mint for oil.

The Bureau of Reclamation, while being the foster parent of the largest share of this agricultural cornucopia, has been subject to criticism by even the farmers themselves. On the Columbia Basin Project, irrigators began to request changes in the regulations governing the size of holding per family almost from the outset of settlement. Insufficient ground to maximize equipment investments was one of the most often repeated justifications for this change. The request seemed to have some foundation, as many operators legally acquired more land to farm by leasing and sometimes not so legally by other means. The system of family-sized farms, that was insisted on by the Bureau for the settlement of the Columbia Basin, seemed to be nostalgically rooted in the past and a homesteading scheme.

It arrived on the economic-agricultural scene precisely at the time that was marked by the national trend of increasing farm size. Furthermore, the notion that equivalence (more or less) in all farm income on the project could be manipulated by making small farms of those areas having good soils and large farms from areas having poor soils was clearly a mistake. The point of diminishing returns for the areas of poorer soils seems to have been misjudged. While the original acreage limitations have been increased, there is still pressure for even greater relaxation of these restrictions.

Regardless of the land economics problems, the irrigated specialty crops of the region provide it with both fame and fortune as they are consumed throughout the nation.

Dairying. To the casual observer, the specialization of dairying is probably the least impressive agricultural endeavor. The common sight of cows grazing on the permanent pasture of western Washington and Oregon belies both its local and regional significance. Dairy products consistently rank high in the value of agricultural production for each state in the region. Washington produces the most milk, while Idaho is the most important source of cheese, despite the fact that Oregon's production is more prestigious. Milk production in Washington and Idaho is significantly greater per cow than the national average—the local dairymen somehow managing to obtain greater quantities of milk from a smaller number of animals. The mysteries of this aspect of agricultural intensification have never been revealed to this observer.

The pattern of milksheds associated with the urban centers of the region is as one would expect, with the exception of Seattle. Since it is coexistent with an area of dairying concentration, it is a source of these products as well as a market. Dairy products, including fresh milk, are sometimes shipped from this western area to the east of the Cascades, providing a slight reversal in the usual flow pattern of milksheds.

The dairying adaptation to the Marine West Coast climate of this region is similar to that found in Europe, the original source for the most common milk-producing cows. The combination of temperature and precipitation are such that pasture grasses grow almost continuously. The necessity for outbuildings for animal shelter is minimal, as is winter feeding. Outside of this western area of the region, the other areas of concentration are limited to the milksheds and places where irrigation is an important phase of the agricultural land use.

Livestock Raising. The raising of livestock in this region is still more like that of the Old West than the feed lots of the Central United States, although change along those lines is occurring in the lower Columbia Basin. The large expanses of natural grasslands of the prairies and the unsettled mountain valleys provide the space for the oldest agricultural practice in the West. This part of the region's livelihood, more than any other, preserves the characteristics of the Western life style. This should not be construed to mean that all the cattle are still rounded up by cowboys on horseback, however, for as incongruous as it may seem the Honda motorcycle has become the favored steed of many ranch men.

Idaho is the principal producer of beef, followed by Oregon, Washington, and western Montana. This same ranking holds true for sheep and lambs as well. The region generally produces about 5 percent of the nation's supply of cattle and calves.

Sheep and lamb production has been declining gradually over the years, and farm flocks now tend to be more common than range flocks. It was inevitable in the settlement of the region that livestock grazing would be subordinate to cultivated agricultural crops, so time has seen lands used for grazing pushed farther and farther to the edges of the cropland. As a result of better price increases for beef than sheep, the lands utilized by sheep are becoming fewer as well as the most marginal. If a circular form is assumed, a sort of zonation of land use intensity results, which places sheep on the periphery, beef in the next zone, cropland in the next, and the more intensive suburban and urban uses in the center.

A cattle breeding industry of more than modest proportions has continually provided the means for refining and perpetuating a valuable Northwestern livestock industry. Increased local beef production will probably be required to meet the demands of the growing region.

Agricultural Processing. One of the most rapidly growing segments of the regional economy is food processing. While canning factories for the vegetable and fruit crops of the region have long existed in the centers associated with that production, newly irrigated lands and their resulting crops in addition to innovations in food processing have caused further expansion in regional food processing. Sugar refineries, potato processing plants, cold apple storage, frozen food preparations, and dehydrated dairy products all have appeared on the scene on a larger scale in the very recent past.

Freezing and dehydration have been important improvements in food handling for the Northwestern agriculturist for they are now able to tap a large U.S. market as well as open a new one within the region.

Food processing for the region's livestock industry is becoming more important, too, as farmers realize the value of concentrated winter feeds and starter meals for young animals.

A list of agricultural products undergoing regional food processing would look like a supermarket's Saturday sale sheet for they run the gamut from fruits to flour. The increasing importance of this industry is yet another indication that the region is outgrowing its adolescence.

Wheat, beef, sugar, apples—what does it all add up to? From this observer's point of view, a massive, intricate, profitable industry. The farm operators of the Northwest enjoy one of the highest level-of-living indexes of the whole nation, and they remain quite independent in their success. Unlike the South and Midwest, most farms and ranches are owner-operated. The combination of homesteading, youth, and reclamation irrigation produces a pattern of individual ownership quite in contrast to the higher levels of tenantry elsewhere. As a matter of fact, the proportion of tenantry in Northwestern agriculture has constantly declined since 1920.

Sufficient water of good quality exists to expand irrigation agriculture, particularly in Idaho, but the region must certainly be close to the end of its reservoir of convertible lands. This fact should cause an even closer look at the regional economic balance sheet to determine the emphasis for the next stage of development.

FISHERIES

An overall decline is perceptible in the number and value of the Northwestern fish catch, and a gradual shift to Alaskan waters has been going on for years. Overfishing, pollution, and large hydroelectric dams have all contributed to this decline.

Salmon, the region's fish of greatest commercial value, is now sought as keenly by the sports fishermen as by the commercial fishermen. As anadromous fish, part of the salmon's life cycle is spent in the freshwater streams where life began for them. At some special time, they commence a journey to the sea performing a kind of transhumance to the ocean pastures. When adults, the fish begin the journey back from whence they came, and if not netted, hooked, or preyed on in some other manner, upon reaching their rearing place, a male and female salmon perform their separate reproductive functions, and the species is perpetuated.

Over the past five years the average value of the commercial fisherman's catch of principal species in Washington and Oregon combined has been approximately equivalent to Washington's egg production ($22 to $25 million). When the food processing industry is finished with the fish, however, the value has more than doubled. The value of Oregon's sports fishery is estimated to be almost three times the value of its commercial fishery.

The value of the regional catch is approximately 6 percent of the value of production in the United States. Since 1945 a decline has occurred in the annual regional catch, but this has been offset somewhat by an increase in value. How long this increased value can perpetuate intensive commercial exploitation is still a matter of speculation. Indications are that there will be continued commercial fishing pressure in response to rising prices and still greater sports fishery activity.

Regional fish exports are primarily to California and the Midwest. About 65 percent of the groundfish are shipped to California in the form of fresh fillets while approximately 35 percent of the fresh salmon caught regionally are shipped to the Midwest. Regional markets consume the remainder of these catches. There are practically no international exports of fish from the region because of its poor competitive position compared to the East Coast fishery and foreign producers. Seattle is still the most important fishing port of the region, handling the greatest share of both processing and packing.

With the advent of larger and more reliable boats and outboard motors, the safety factor of coastal sports fishing has improved considerably, and a whole new flotilla has been added to the salmon fishery. About one in four adult residents of Washington owns a boat of some description and if the "value added" by installment contracts could be identified, the sports fishery would no doubt rank quite high as an income generating industry. Expenditures by regional salmon and steelhead fishermen alone are estimated at $100 million per year. The places where the Northwestern fishermen go to sea have been improved and modernized over the years as have the fish handling facilities.

Problems. Pollution problems are associated principally with oxygen consuming residues that are added to the fresh waters of the states. Water temperature is also a critical factor for the migrating anadromous fish and industrial processes often can alter the natural condition of the stream to the point that a fish is incapable of performing his reproductive rites. Nuclear electric generation plans of the future, which include the use of surface streams for cooling purposes, must obviously take into account their capacity for environmental alteration of the aquatic circumstances of the region.

Great efforts have been made to accommodate the anadromous fish since the industry they support is long standing and has economic significance at least on a local scale. Whether their preservation in the regional waters will continue to cause a future foregoing of other economic benefits that might accrue, particularly in the field of electrical energy, is unpredictable. A concerted effort could be made to rejuvenate and reserve numerous small coastal streams for purposes of fish rearing in conjunction with a few of the larger inland streams that already represent large investments for fish passage facilities. In any case, it should be clear that any dollar and cents evaluation that is critical of the existence of the fishing industry will serve only to alert the Northwestern populace to the state of affairs and the alternatives. An economic evaluation is simply not taken as the equivalent of a mandate for political action by the "Association of Amalgamated Conservateurs of the Northwestern States."

Indian fishing rights granted to tribes by their treaties with the United States are a very real source of trouble within the region. Washington's coastal Indians have sometimes reacted violently to state regulatory provisions concerning stream closures and catching methods. The use of firearms to prevent trespass of even state officials on traditional Indian fishing grounds has not been uncommon. Compromise is difficult to accomplish for the Indians expect the contracts represented by their treaties to be valid for all time. The state's position is that citizens should obey regulations whose design is to perpetuate goods for the benefit of all and that non-navigable streams are subject to state regulation. Invalid assumptions have been made on both sides, which continue to propel the entire situation toward an unwanted confrontation. The state appears to believe that the Indian willfully desires to fish himself right out of business by using the easiest and most effective (and therefore illegal) means of catching the fish. In other words, for some reason the conservation of fish at the traditional Indian fishing sites is only an idea that the state or white man understands. The Indian, on the other hand, refuses, in his somewhat rightful intolerance, to be intimidated by the forces of change brought about by time. Untouched by the main thrust of economic and socio-political improvement, the Indian is understandably adamant to give in to its pressures or to those that share the responsibility for his nonparticipation. So long as treaties were made investing the rights of fishing in perpetuity, he can justifiably insist that the citizens of the United States must honor their obligations in perpetuity—and that is a long time.

Concern over competition on the high seas with both the Japanese and Russian fishing fleets has been the cause for international conferences on the fishery of the Pacific Basin. The American Pacific fishing fleet can expect increasing competition from these rapidly expanding and highly mechanized fleets of her western neighbors.

TRANSPORTATION EQUIPMENT

As a non-resource-oriented industry, the manufacture of transportation equipment is unusual in the Pacific Northwest. By whatever measure, the aircraft industry (which for all practical purposes is the Boeing Aircraft Corporation of Seattle) is the most important segment of the industry. Using aluminum produced locally this one firm is marketing over $2 billion worth of aircraft to the government and airline customers annually. The Boeing Company began inauspiciously by making small aircraft from the spruce available nearby and has grown into the manufacture of the most sophisticated transportation devices of the aerospace industries.

Practically all the activity associated with this industry is located in the Willamette-Puget Trough. The Bremerton Naval Shipyards have been a continuing source of employment and will soon be undergoing alterations for nuclear ship facilities. Tugs and barges utilized in the coastal and Columbia River trades as well as freight cars are manufactured in Portland. The port handling facilities at Portland and Seattle are adjusting rapidly to the new mode of freight containerization, and detachable truck-trailers can be seen being loaded onto ships especially fitted for such cargo. The increased flexibility of this method of shipment has decreased dock loading and handling, providing such benefits as fresh fruits and vegetables to Alaskans more cheaply and all year around.

SUMMARY

The employment of the region's resources in a gainful manner has resulted in a defined pattern of land uses, each of which reconfirms the generalization that the Northwest is in only the beginning stages of economic maturity.

With the already heavy investment made in the agricultural industries, it seems reasonable to assume that it will retain its importance, and, as regional population increases, its role will attain even greater significance. This should provide greater diversity and cause some expansion in the agricultural processing industries, thereby continuing the progression of economic development in that segment of the economy.

The importance of the electrical industry, forestry, and the water resources no doubt will dominate the character of the regional output of manufacturing and industrial development for some time. While some bemoan the characteristics and state of development of the region's industries, others declare it most compatible with their mental image of a desirable place to live. Some regional residents find it unbecoming to live in a semi-colonial state, while others hail the situation as being much less onerous than one dominated by numerous blighting industries and all those people that would accompany them.

6   *Commerce—Transport*
         and Trade

I N THE earliest days of Northwestern settlement, water transportation was the most important mode of heavy transport.
It moved people, lumber, and staples along the coast from California
to Alaska and up and down the lower reaches of the Columbia
River. Sternwheel steamships plied various sections of this stream,
separated by rapids that were not negotiable except when the combination of high water, high steam, and a high spirited captain occurred simultaneously. In 1856, the Indians were still trying to
prevent the settling incursion represented by the steamboats on the
Columbia.

Rail Transport. Today, railroads are the prime movers insofar
as the Northwestern States are concerned for they combine an adequate network of internal and external linkages with a hauling
capacity that is adaptable to all kinds of freight. California is the
region's most favored neighbor as it represents the destination of
nearly 30 percent of the region's outbound goods traveling by rail.
There is some reciprocity in this traffic, since the region is the recipient of about 20 percent of California's outbound rail tonnage.

Naturally, the greatest extent of outbound goods are products of
the highly localized, resource oriented Northwestern industries. As
such, they are characteristically bulky items of relatively low per
unit value and are favored in rail commerce by a commodity rate
that is lower than the class rates applied to finished goods being shipped into the region. These lower rates are important factors in the

ability of Northwestern goods to compete in the markets of the United States. It has been estimated that an average ton of rail freight which terminates in the state of Washington and one which originates there, also, will travel 84 percent farther than the national average for freight between its points of origin and destination.[19] It is not difficult to see that the Northwestern consumer in his cost of living expenses is to some degree subsidizing the region's industries whose markets are in Chicago and points east. Rail car shortages for both outbound commodities and intraregional traffic often occur because of the extent of outbound shipping and the fact that most inbound goods do not require as much space as their counterparts in regional commerce.

Washington has the highest density of railroad track mileage, expressed in miles of track per square area, followed by Oregon, Montana, and Idaho. Washington's density figure (.07 miles per square mile) is more than double that of each of its neighbors.

There has been a steady decline in the total rail line mileage in the Pacific Northwest since 1940 as minor branch lines have been abandoned. One of the few places in the region where new trackage is being laid is in the lower Columbia Basin where the demand for heavy transportation equipment associated with agricultural production has increased.

To date, the rail transportation industry of the Pacific Northwest has gone through three phases. The transition from the normal size steam engine to the mammoth Malley engine took place in the late 1930s. Due to the increased size of this newer engine, fewer of them were required to haul the same amount of freight. They were responsible for almost doubling the number of cars that could be pulled by their smaller counterparts. These new engines required fewer stops for water and maintenance, which resulted in a decline in the number of railroad "whistle stops." The increased freight capacities of these trains, however, caused an increase in the handling facilities at

[19] *Trends in Distribution, Services and Transportation with Particular Reference to Washington,* Economics and Business Studies Bulletin #4 (Pullman: Washington State University, College of Economics & Business, 1966).

terminal points, which contributed to the urban and industrial growth of these locations. In the late 1940s, the Malley engine was superseded by the modern diesel electrics. Using a more flexible source of power, these diesel engines required even less in the way of in-transit maintenance, and their adoption provided the demise of railroad coal yards and water towers throughout the region. This second phase ushered in the third phase as railroad yard trackage increased and even larger switching facilities became necessary to handle the greater quantities of freight. This change is exemplified by the automated gravity switching yard located at Pasco, Washington.

Many parts of the region owe their existence to the necessity of transportation (as discussed in Chapter 3). The nucleating effect of the regional transportation system is still evolving as the merger of the Great Northern, Northern Pacific, Burlington and Spokane, Portland, and Seattle railways into the "Great Northern Pacific and Burlington" will result in Portland, Oregon, being the West Coast center of four transcontinental railroad lines (Northern Pacific, Southern Pacific, Great Northern, and Milwaukee). When this increased rail freight capacity is coupled with the rapid expansion of the Portland shipping facilities, it produces a pattern of ever increasing importance for the city as a regional transportation node.

Highway System. The main road system of the Pacific Northwest, consisting of the federal interstate and primary state highways, provides adequate internal and external access for the region. U.S. Highways numbers 2, 10, 30, and 20 cross the region in an east-west direction and constitute particularly important linkages in Washington and Oregon where they connect the disparate halves of those two states. U.S. 10 is the most important link between Seattle and Spokane and will soon be the first multiple lane road to span Washington from east to west. U.S. 20 in Oregon connects the southern part of Idaho with the lower Willamette Valley.

In a north-south direction, there are six highways that cross the region, but three, U.S. 99, 97, and 395, are the most important. Almost all of the mileage of U.S. 99 within the region is a multiple lane road and it carries the highest density of traffic. Located in the Willamette Puget Lowland, it connects the main urban and industrial centers of the region.

Washington has the highest percentage of municipal road mileage and also the greatest density of highway mileage, with Oregon and Idaho following. As would be expected, the natural landscape has been an important influence on the nature of the distribution of the transport network. Mountainous central Idaho, arid southeastern Oregon, and mountainous north central Washington are all regions exhibiting voids insofar as transport systems are concerned. Water level routes and low mountain passes played important roles in the location of portions of the grid.

Changes in the intensity of the road network of the region have been spectacular. Since 1950, Oregon has doubled its road mileage, with Washington and Idaho showing increases of about 70 percent. Northwestern increases in truck, bus, and automobile traffic have kept pace proportionately with the rest of the nation. Its largest cities and their environs exhibit characteristics of highway congestion that are similar to those of other regions.

Seaports and Trade. Since its early settlement, water transportation by way of the sea has been an important aspect of the Northwestern region's commerce. It should be stressed, however, that this trade is of primarily local significance. As of 1966, Northwestern exports accounted for about 5 percent of the value of the nation's total exports and 4 percent of its imports.

Wheat and other grains, logs and products of the forest industry are the largest components of regional exports by value, followed by machinery, copper and copper alloys, and aluminum and aluminum alloys. Principal foreign recipients are Canada, Japan, India, and Pakistan. The value of Northwestern exports in 1966 was $1.6 billion, which was about double the figure for 1956.

Import traffic is chiefly from Canada, Japan, the Philippines, South America, and West Germany. Its 1966 value was approximately $1 billion with motor vehicles, plywood veneer, copper ore, chemical products, and iron and steel plate heading the list.

Portland, Seattle, Tacoma, and Longview are the principal ports of the region, accounting for 86 percent of the total waterborne traffic. Coos Bay, Vancouver, and Bellingham account for the remaining 14 percent. Both Portland and Seattle are increasing their public expenditures to improve their ports. Their sailing schedules list many ports and harbors of the world as their destinations with Japan, Western Europe, and South America being the most frequented. The predominance of Japan as a northwestern trade partner has been the result of an interregional complementarity that existed even prior to World War II. With this Asian country becoming an important, world-wide commercial nation and the possibility for increased Pacific Basin trade opportunities, it would behoove the Northwest to provide a western access point to the North American continent. With the advent of container shipping, it is not difficult to picture the United States as a great land bridge between Asia and Europe. In addition to providing a linkage of continental proportions, the region could add its own characteristics of consumption and production to the flow of world goods across its span. It may be that the greatest days of transcontinental shipping are yet to come for the domestic freight movers and dock workers of the Pacific Northwest.

Inland Waterways. Inland waterways of the region are not extensive, being limited to the Columbia-Snake River system and the Willamette River. Navigational locks built in conjunction with the large dams on the Columbia and Snake will eventually provide slack water navigation from Bonneville Dam on the Columbia to Lewiston, Idaho, on the Snake River. There are approximately 340 miles on the Columbia system at present, provided at a yearly operation and maintenance cost of about $5 million. Inland waterways freight consists of wheat, forest industries goods, and products of the agricultural and petroleum industries on the Columbia, while pulp and paper products, rafted logs, sand, gravel, and crushed stone make up the principal freight of the Willamette. Total regional waterway traffic amounts to about one-fourth of that of the Ohio River, at present, but the entire southern side of the richest wheat producing area of the region will be available to inland water transportation when dams on the lower middle portion of the Snake River are completed. This will no doubt be the cause of a renewed economic vigor locally.

Airways. The importance of air transportation within the region has been limited to passenger traffic almost entirely as Northwestern markets and commodities and air transport costs seem to be mutually exclusive. The value of regional air freight shipments accounts for only 2 percent of the exports and 3 percent of the imports. Change may be in the offing in this aspect of commerce, however, as the region's wide open spaces provide two of the major requirements for the new supersonic transport air carriers—few concentrations of people to complain of the noise and the necessary space for airfields and approaches. Deactivated military air bases and preserves are scattered about in the region. It is within the realm of possibility that some portion of the region could become the western hub of a national air transport hierarchy from which international supersonic travelers and goods would be transshipped to their ultimate destinations after being deposited at the regional center.

Air travel service to and within the region has reached a reasonable level considering the regional requirements. An internal network of commuter service between the major regional centers is developing and will provide improved intraregional economic communication.

The Northwest, like any other region, is dependent on an economic mode of transportation to connect it with the core of national activity. Increased regional product mobility provided by less expensive and more extensive transportation systems is important, too, for the regional inhabitants then experience increased accessibility to the goods and services produced by the national economy.

As a region whose economic maturity has not yet been achieved, the Northwestern States can expect to undergo major changes in those aspects that are most important to its development. Commerce and the transportation system that provides its basis are almost certain to be two of the most dynamic features of the future growth of the region.

The Region in Perspective

———————————————————

THIS BOOK has had the character of a corporate progress report in many of its places, which hopefully is indicative of perception and reaction rather than literary style. The impact of progress is strong and fresh here, and its description is a natural task for a book which purports to be about the region. This landscape has undergone such rapid change that, unlikely as it may seem, it is even possible for a regional inhabitant of only four decades to have achieved a degree of historical perspective.

This observer sees the region as an environmental entity characterized by the qualities of being Western, retarded, new and pristine, functional, egocentric, and spiritual. Its Western imagery is more Will Rogers than John Wayne, more Woody Guthrie rather than Roy Rogers. Its retardation contributed to, and is personified by, the failure of the West Coast edition of *The New York Times,* which was cancelled for the lack of interest. In its newness, the region is more Canadian than Alaskan, and functionally it is more like Chicago than Paris. It is more Irish than Italian in its state personality, and its spiritualness is more of the Redwoods than of Rome.

The Social Triad and a Divided Region. Seattle, Spokane, and Portland from a social triad from which Northwestern society emerges. They personify the division of the region, and a digression of characteristics will suffice to elucidate the point. Seattle and Portland are West, Spokane is East. Seattle probably has more conservationist-recreationists per capita than any city in the nation. It is Boeing, Mount Rainier, umbrellas, and the home of the late Theodore Roethke. Some say it has vaulting ambition. It is more San Francisco than Los Angeles.

Portland is a harbor but not a seaport. Its name was settled by the flip of a coin (Boston or Portland), but its New England beginnings are now only a heritage. It has gone about its cultural maturing more sedately if less expansively than Seattle.

The life of its Inland Empire is Spokane's main interest. News of the world is imported and Little Orphan Annie tends to be more venerated than Pogo. Spokane is *the* center of eastern regional opinion, which in law is more J. Edgar Hoover than Earl Warren and in philosophy more Eric Hoffer than Mortimer Adler.

A certain stoicism is discernible among the landed people of the east, which is epitomized by the following excerpt from an agricultural report from the Yakima Valley, Washington: "High winds visited the valley on Thursday and did some damage by uprooting trees, blowing roofs from buildings, blowing down power lines, and spreading trash fires to buildings and haystacks." All in a day's work!

Purposeful Change. The political basis for the economic growth of the region has been dominated almost continuously by the idea of public works. The social investments beginning in the 1930s started new life in the soil and among the people and caused economic ripple marks of ever-widening scope and intensity.

The greatest regional challenge amounts to a state of mind: preparedness for change. Being one of the nation's most youthful parts has been advantageous, for this circumstance has permitted the developmental history of other regions to be reviewed from the sanctuary of the Northwestern land cradle. Change has been slow and purposeful with momentum gathering internally rather than externally. The time has passed when the region's development could be determined solely from within its borders, however. The inevitability of becoming an active part of the nation's sociological scheme renders the region vulnerable to national needs and demands and will soon cause the neophyte region to take on some extra-regional responsibilities.

Even though the region is now subject to the propulsion of a myriad of political, economic, and social forces, it need not repeat the mistakes of other regions. While compatibility may be negotiable between alternative land uses, planning facilities must be provided to identify and recommend from among the choices. To endure the problems engendered by lethargic governments, environmental pollution, and the special pleading of certain interest groups is a heavy price for the people and the environment to pay for not preparing for guided change.

One of the most important area needs is a good introspective stare at its egocentric regional attitudes. Some of them often prevent a realistic assessment of the nature of regional relationships with important and needy neighbors and cause anachronisms that defy explanation. For example, a scheme of "sister cities" between the Northwest and Japan was introduced recently, the purpose of which was to promote trade and goodwill. Shortly thereafter came the suggestion for a prohibition against log exports from the region's public forests to Japan. The small steel industry of the Northwest would like the legislature of Washington to enact trade reciprocity laws to protect its local market and start a "buy American" campaign that would very likely seriously hamper other local industries that have customers in many foreign countries. California, an even closer neighbor and important market for Northwestern goods and services and a large source of tourist income, is hardly accorded courteous replies to its requests for assistance in solving its electrical and water problems, despite the fact that the Northwestern water developments occurred under federal, not state or regional, auspices. Regional nationalism does not provide a basis for sound economic growth and the Northwest should cease indulging in it.

Regional Problems. Aside from external relations, there are three categories of internal problems that represent significant challenges to the future. First, there are impending social problems which trouble the conscience of other than just the regional inhabitants. The Northwestern Indian, the Negro, and other minority groups share the common insult of reservation living. Rapid progress is needed to deter any further exposure of these people to the debilitating effects of inadequate social mobility.

The problems caused by urban growth call for more and better regional planning. Suburban developments, which grow rapidly and demand automobile access to the adjacent urban cores, sometimes force a pattern of settlement on the environment that is both chaotic and ugly. By far the greatest increases of pressure on the land created by continued population growth will occur in the Willamette-Puget Trough. Knowing this, efforts should be made via regional plans to propose settlement concepts that strive to provide an ecological balance between the people's requirement for living space and regional beauty.

The second category of problems has an economic orientation. Underdeveloped regional markets will continue to plague local manufacturers as long as the area remains underpopulated. While the extractive based industries do provide a relatively stable economic foundation, increased business and manufacturing require greater diversification and access to wider markets. Current trends in the transportation equipment industry are indications of favorable activity in this regard. Increased demands for power in a region that already has a consumption rate three times greater than the national average require continued diligence in the field of water resource development. Fewer sites for hydroelectric installations and favorable development costs for nuclear generated power will probably usher in the Northwestern atomic age and its attendant problems in the next decade.

Irrigation agriculture can be expected to continue to expand, particularly in southern Idaho, but a serious review of the homestead orientation of the Bureau of Reclamation is probably in order. While it may seem unusual for the Bureau to support plantation agriculture, its development policies should not entirely ignore the current economic character of the agricultural production enterprise.

Lastly, greater problems of a physical nature will be confronting the region in the very near future. Pollution of the air and water in this region has already reached the critical stage in some localities. Missoula, Montana's "Big Sky Country," is often obscured by atmospheric pollutants of the forest industries. With industry and manufacturing just beginning to be important facets of the region's economic scheme, it is not encouraging to note the extent of pollution difficulties already being encountered. Conflicts in resource utilization and preservation will no doubt occur with greater regularity and intensity as the wide open spaces become less open.

The closeness of the past is a regional characteristic that most of its inhabitants enjoy very much, as it is a source for a mode of behavior that is still admired. The charisma of the West, therefore, is probably somewhat responsible for inhibiting the region's progress. But as it grows past adolescence, the region will sweep its areal segments and people along toward maturity. Not uniformly, of course, as "parts of it will remain innocent for some time to come."

Suggestions for Additional Reading

Atwood, Wallace W. *The Physiographic Provinces of North America.* Waltham, Massachusetts: Ginn and Company, 1940.

Baldwin, Ewart M. *Geology of Oregon.* Eugene, Oregon: University of Oregon, 1959.

Bessey, Roy F. *Pacific Northwest Regional Planning—A Review.* Olympia, Washington: Department of Conservation, 1963.

Brier, Howard. *Sawdust Empire—The Pacific Northwest.* New York: Alfred Knopf, 1958.

Brimlow, G. F. *Harney County Oregon and its Rangeland.* Portland, Oregon: Binsford and Mort, 1951.

Brogan, P. F. *East of the Cascades.* Portland, Oregon: Binsford and Mort, 1964.

Campbell, Charles D. *Introduction to Washington Geology and Resources.* Washington Department of Conservation, Division of Mines and Geology, 1962.

Clawson, Marion. *Uncle Sam's Acres.* New York: Dodd, Mead and Company, 1951.

Freeman, Otis and Martin, Howard. *The Pacific Northwest.* New York; Wiley and Company, 1954. Second edition.

Haystead, Ladd and Fite, Gilbert. *The Agricultural Regions of the United States.* University of Oklahoma Press, 1955.

Highsmith, R. M. (editor). *Atlas of the Pacific Northwest.* Corvallis, Oregon: Oregon State University Press, 1962. Third edition.

Holbrook, Stewart. *The Columbia.* New York: Rinehart, 1956.

Johansen, D. O. *Empire of the Columbia.* New York: Harper, 1957.

Krutilla, John V. *The Columbia River Treaty; The Economics of an International River Basin Development.* Baltimore, Maryland: Johns Hopkins Press, 1967.

110

———— *Sequence and Timing in River Basin Development.* Baltimore, Maryland: Johns Hopkins Press, 1967.

———— and Ekstein, Otto. *Multiple Purpose River Development.* Baltimore, Maryland: Johns Hopkins Press, 1958.

McKinley, Charles. *Uncle Sam in the Pacific Northwest.* Berkeley, California: University of California Press, 1952.

Morgan, Murray. *The Columbia, Powerhouse of the West.* Seattle, Washington: Superior Publishing Company, 1949.

Pomeroy, Earl. *The Pacific Slope.* New York: Alfred Knopf, 1965.

Sundborg, George. *Hail Columbia.* New York: Macmillan and Company, 1954.

Index

113